OSPREY MILITARY CA

ASPERN

Left and centre: Hungarian officer and private of IR51 (Splenyi). As part of Grenadier Battalion Scharlach this unit took part in the bloody storming of the Granary and Great Garden at Essling on 22 May 1809. Right: Nine battalions of Austrian jager were formed in 1808. A third of each battalion was armed wth rifles as illustrated, although the uniform, described as 'pike-grey', was more blue-grey than shown here. (Bryan Fosten)

GENERAL EDITOR DAVID G. CHANDLER

OSPREY MILITARY **CAMPAIGN SERIES** **33**

ASPERN & WAGRAM 1809

MIGHTY CLASH OF EMPIRES

IAN CASTLE

First published in Great Britain 1994 by OSPREY an imprint of Reed Consumer Books Limited, Michelin House, 81 Fulham Road, London SW3 6RB and Aukland, Melbourne, Singapore and Toronto.

Reprinted 1995
ISBN 1-85532-366-4

Produced by DAG Publications Ltd for Osprey Publishing Ltd.
Colour bird's eye view illustrations by Peter Harper.
Cartography by Micromap.
Wargaming the 1809 Campaign by Ian Drury
Mono camerawork by M&E Reproductions, North Fambridge, Essex.
Printed and bound in Hong Kong.

▶ *Wagram, first day. At 9.00 p.m. in heavy rain, troops began crossing the river on bridges that had been prepared in advance. In this illustration the nearest bridge is that used by Davout's Corps; the second bridge is that constructed to carry Massena's cavalry and artillery across. In the background the burning village of Gross-Enzersdorf can be seen. (K. Foresman).*

Key to Map Symbols

Army Group	xxxxx ⊠
Army	xxxx ⊠
Corps	xxx ⊠
Division	xx ⊠
Brigade	x ⊠
Regiment	lll ⊠
Battalion	ll ⊠
Infantry	⊠
Cavalry	◣
Artillery	•

▶ *A bird's eye view of the Marchfeld on the first day of the Battle of Wagram. The French corps fan out across the plain and move towards the awaiting Austrian line. Lobau island and the bridges are in the left foreground, while the village of Deutsch-Wagram is located in the centre background, indicated by the large plume of smoke. (Musée de l'Armée, Paris).*

CONTENTS

Private of Fusiliers Chasseurs (left) and Corporal of Fusiliers Grenadiers (right). These men of the Young Guard took part in the desperate fighting that raged through the village of Essling and at Wagram they were ordered to support Macdonald's shattered square. (Bryan Fosten)

THE ROAD TO WAR, 1809

After victories in the campaigns of 1805, 1806 and 1807, Napoleon Bonaparte was at the height of his power. All continental Europe had witnessed the strength of his sword; now the only thorn in his side was Britain, who continued to finance and encourage the aggressive intentions of his enemies. To reduce British influence and destroy its economy, Napoleon introduced his Continental System, a Europe-wide trade ban on British goods. Portugal, an old ally of Britain, had declared herself neutral during Europe's disturbances but was only too happy to open the port of Lisbon to British shipping. But by late November 1807, the loophole had been closed, Portugal having been occupied by Napoleon, with Spanish support.

Napoleon's ambition, however, did not rest there. Using the occupation of Portugal as a means to advance more French troops into Spain, under the pretext that they were necessary to support his forces there, he considerably strengthened his position in the Iberian peninsula.

The population of Spain soon became agitated by the growing foreign presence in their country, and outbreaks of disorder there gave Napoleon the opportunity to place his brother, Joseph, on the Spanish throne. In no time disorder became rioting, and the population rose against the French. In July 1808 a French army was forced to surrender to the Spanish at Bailen; shortly afterwards a small British army landed in Portugal and defeated a French force at Vimiero. The defeat and surrender of these two forces caused a sensation throughout Europe– and in Vienna's corridors of power it was just the news they had been waiting for.

Austria Awakens

Austria had been the most steadfast of all France's opponents since the early days of the Revolution. Under Francis II, the Habsburg ruler of the Holy Roman Empire, Austria had first fought against France between 1792 and 1797 but had been defeated following Napoleon's conquest of northern Italy and some French success on the Rhine. Austria was at war again within two years, from 1799 to 1801 before being forced to sue for peace after defeat in Bavaria and reverses in Italy. Continuing French expansion caused Austria to launch itself once more on the road to war in 1805, but a humbling surrender at Ulm, followed by the defeat of a joint Russo-Austrian army at Austerlitz, soon brought the campaign to a close. The terms of the ensuing peace were particularly galling for Austria: the removal of her influence in Italy was combined with the elimination of Habsburg power in Germany, leading to the dissolution of the Holy Roman Empire. The numerous states that had made up this ancient empire were reorganized as the Confederation of the Rhine, now to become a French protectorate. Francis II, no longer Holy Roman Emperor, would henceforth be Emperor Francis I of Austria. Undaunted, Austria began to rebuild its army, awaiting a favourable opportunity to regain its former position of power and influence in Europe.

The threatening situation in Spain and rumours that Austria was rearming caused Napoleon much concern. At a conference in September 1808 he persuaded the Russian Tsar, Alexander I, to support him should Austria declare war on France. Satisfied with this, Napoleon ordered the transfer of 200,000 men from Germany to Spain, where he himself proceeded to deal with the increasingly vexing situation in the west.

In Austria the leading political and military figures debated the situation. After much discussion it was agreed that the time was right to gain revenge for the losses of 1805: support was promised by Britain and Prussia, and there was the prospect of France being weakened by the escalating conflict in Spain. So a decision was taken to prepare for a new war to begin in the spring of 1809.

OPPOSING COMMANDERS

Archduke Charles (Erzherzog Karl)

Charles, aged 38 in 1809, had first seen military action as a Generalmajor (the rank a privilege of birth) in 1793 at the victories over the French at Aldenhoven and Neerwinden. These successes led to his rapid promotion to the rank of Feldmarschall Leutnant and a command at the Austrian defeat at Fleures before a recurrence of the ill health that plagued him for much of his life caused him to resign from the army and embark on the first of his military writings. Unimpressed by the way his aged seniors had handled the army, he then manoeuvred his way to command of the Army of the Rhine in the campaign of 1796, at the age of 25. His success in southern Germany was tempered by French gains in Italy. The delay in transferring Charles to the disintegrating southern front ensured victory

◄ *Archduke Charles (1771–1847) was a younger brother of the Habsburg Emperor Francis I. He first saw service in 1793 and commanded an Army when only 25 years old. Charles was a great military reformer and theorist but did not always receive the full support of the Emperor. He displayed great personal bravery during the campaign and became the first general to defeat Napoleon in battle. (Heeresgeschichtliches Museum, Vienna).*

▲ Left to right, top to bottom:

GdK Heinrich Count Bellegarde was 53 in 1809 and had joined the army in 1976. He had served with Charles in 1776, when some tension developed between them. In 1805 he commanded the Austrian centre at Caldiero. In the 1809 campaign, he was appointed commander of I Korps and was described as a 'gallant man and an extremely brave soldier, but lacking the enterprise required of a field commander'. (HGM, Vienna).

FZM Carl Count Kolowrat-Krakowsky was 61 in 1809. He had joined the army in 1764 and was a veteran of the Turkish Wars. In 1801 he was appointed head of the Interior Ministry and shortly after he served as military commander in Bohemia. At Austerlitz in 1805 he held joint command of one of the main attacking columns and in 1809 he was to command II Korps. (HGM, Vienna).

FML Freidrich Xavier Prince Hohenzollern-Hechingen, born in Maastrict in 1757, had first seen service in 1779 and had served with Charles in Italy in 1797. In 1805 he had distinguished himself by cutting his way out of the encirclement at Ulm with his men. With his reputation as a reliable commander intact, he entered the 1809 campaign at the head of III Korps. (HGM, Vienna).

FML Johann Baron Hiller, the only corps commander not a member of the old high aristocracy, had been with the army since 1763. He had served with Charles in Italy in 1796 and was wounded at Zurich in 1799. In 1809, Hiller was appointed commander of VI Korps, but disagreements with Charles led to some animosity between the two that was never far below the surface. (HGM, Vienna).

GdK Johann, Prince Liechtenstein, had quickly proved himself a fine cavalry commander, serving under Charles in 1796 and again in 1799, distinguishing himself at Stockach; his reputation was further enhanced at Hohenlinden in 1800 and Austerlitz in 1805. Charles was close to Liechtenstein personally and professionally. In 1806, when Napoleon had made him a Sovereign Prince of the Confederation of the Rhine, he had chosen to abdicate in favour of his three year old son so that he could continue to serve Austria. (D Hollins).

◀ *'German' and Hungarian Grenadiers. The figure on the left is a member of IR1 (Kaiser Franz), recruited in Moravia, which formed part of the Hohenloe Grenadier Battalion at Aspern and which was renamed the Hromada battalion by the time of Wagram. The figure on the right is from IR19 (Alvinczy) which formed part of the Zetlar Grenadier Battalion. This battalion had been in Italy with Archduke John and arrived at Wagram too late to take part in the battle. (Bryan Fosten)*

for Napoleon, but the later stages of the campaign marked the first occasion when the two generals crossed swords. Signs of tension between Charles and his brother Francis, the emperor, surfaced at this time and continued throughout the rest of Charles' military career, increasing the problems inherent in his already complex position. Charles led his army to victory against the French again at Ostrach and Stockach in 1799 but was again struck down by ill health. Briefly returning, only to experience Francis' displeasure following his

independent actions at Zurich, he again withdrew from the army to his estates in Bohemia.

As Feldmarschall in 1801, Charles returned to the army in a strong position, having avoided involvement in the defeats of 1800, and was given the opportunity to begin a long-needed series of enlightened reforms. These earned him a number of enemies as well as friends. The intrigues that followed placed Baron Mack in command of the army in Germany, which he led to a humiliating surrender at Ulm, thereby negating Charles' own successes in Italy. This defeat of Austria in 1805 finally assured Charles' complete control of the military establishment; he was made Generalissimus in 1806. Unopposed but carefully observed by his brother, Charles returned to his reform programme and formulated a plan to organize his forces on a corps basis along French lines.

Although Charles had gained from his combat experience against the French, and had begun to adopt some of their methods, he was still restricted in the appointment of his senior commanders. In the Habsburg army, progression was dictated more by birth and seniority than by military prowess. Despite this, those who would lead Charles' corps in 1809 were generally steady, experienced men, although prone to internal bickering and lacking in individual initiative.

The Austrian Corps Commanders

General der Kavalerie (GdK) Count Bellegarde, appointed to the command of I Korps, was 53 years old and a member of a noble family from Savoy. He was generally considered one of the better educated generals, sound but unenterprising. II Korps were to be led by 61 year old Feldzeugmeister (FZM) Count Kolowrat-Krakowsky, a Bohemian noble. The command of III Korps was awarded to a Rhineland noble, Feldmarschall Leutnant (FML) Prince Hohenzollern-Hechingen; aged 52 in 1809, he was respected as a reliable leader. FML Prince Rosenberg-Orsini, from a German family of Italian descent, had fought alongside Charles in 1796 and 1805 and now commanded IV Korps. Archduke Louis (Erzherzog Ludwig), appointed as head of V Korps, was 25 years old and a younger brother of Charles and Francis. The only corps commander not of noble birth was FML Baron Hiller of VI Korps. Now aged 61, he had joined the army as a cadet in 1763 and had earned his title during the war against the Turks in 1788–9. Commanding I Reserve Korps was the able cavalry commander and diplomat GdK Prince Liechtenstein, aged 49, whom Charles considered his friend and most able subordinate. The final component of the main army, II Reserve Korps, was entrusted to FML Baron Kienmayer who had been extremely active during the 1805 campaign.

There were also to be two secondary theatres of war, command being handed to further members of the imperial family. GdK Archduke John (Erzherzog Johan), another of Charles' brothers, now aged 27, was to lead the Army of Inner Austria, which comprised VIII and IX Korps, in northern Italy. To the north-east, FML Archduke Ferdinand d'Este, the emperor's 29 year old brother-in-law, was to lead VII Korps in Poland.

Napoleon Bonaparte

The greatest soldier of his age, Napoleon was 40 years old in 1809. He had first come to the public attention in 1793 following the successful siege of Toulon where, as an artillery captain, he had by intrigue and diplomacy been swiftly promoted to Général de brigade. The fast changing political situation in Paris limited subsequent military opportunities, but his loyalty to the Directory eventually rewarded him with command of the Army of Italy, which he led to victory over the Austrians in 1796.

In an effort to restrict British influence and trade, Napoleon advocated a plan to attack Egypt in 1798. Early successes soon turned sour, and with the loss of the French fleet at the Battle of the Nile, Napoleon left his isolated army and returned to France with a handful of selected officers.

Back in France, Napoleon found a country disillusioned with the corrupt Directory and the reverses sustained by the army in the campaigns of 1799. A coup that followed saw Napoleon's star rise again, and within a very short time he had manipulated his way to supreme power as First Consul of France. In the campaign of 1800, French fortunes turned, and new successes in Germany and Italy buoyed the country. The ensuing peace enabled him to turn his attention to improving the administration and economy of France. With great popular support, Napoleon was proclaimed Emperor of the French in May 1804.

The peace was short-lived. A year later Napoleon led his army east and in a whirlwind campaign crushed a Russo-Austrian alliance in 1805. Prussia and Russia formed an alliance the following year; the Prussian Army was defeated at Jena-Auerstädt in 1806, then the Russians at

Friedland in 1807. Within the space of two years Napoleon had defeated the three great powers of the continent leaving him master of Europe.

Napoleon was still the greatest motivator of men, but by 1809 he had begun to believe in his own infallibility. In the forthcoming campaign against Austria he showed himself guilty of overconfidence and the underestimation of his opponents. He deluded himself that the Austrian Army had learnt nothing from its earlier defeats.

French Corps Commanders

Napoleon's subordinates had fought with him across the battlefields of Europe and were all greatly experienced, but at the outbreak of hostilities he was not in Germany. Overall control of the army resting with his Chief of Staff, the 56 year old Maréchal Berthier, whose administrative abilities far outweighed his military skills. The formation in the frontline at the outbreak of war was III Corps under Maréchal Davout; aged 39, he was the son of a cavalry officer of noble descent. Général Oudinot was also in Germany, in temporary command of II Corps. The son of a brewer, he was now 42 years old and had seen much fighting but was to be superseded by Maréchal Lannes, ordered to the new front from Spain. The 40 year old Maréchal had served as an apprentice dyer before joining the army. In France, IV Corps was formed under 51 year old Maréchal Massena, the son of a trader, who was regarded as an able and dogged commander. Maréchal Lefebvre, at 54 the oldest of the corps commanders, was also recalled from Spain on Napoleon's insistence that all corps should be led by French officers; this miller's son was to head the

◀ *Napoleon Bonaparte (1769–1821) is portrayed here in 1805 as King of Italy. Napoleon's rise to power from the Ecole Militaire in Paris to become Emperor of France in 1804 had taken only 20 years. With great victories soon following over Russia and Austria in 1805, Prussia in 1806 and Russia again in 1807, Napoleon entered 1809 as master of Europe. (HGM, Vienna).*

Bavarian VII Corps. The Württemberg troops of VIII Corps were commanded by the 39 year old Général Vandamme, much to the anger of their king, while command of the Saxon IX Corps was handed to Maréchal Bernadotte, aged 46 and the son of a lawyer; he expressed displeasure at his appointment to command the Saxon Army.

Like Austria, France also had troops in the secondary theatres of Italy and Poland; the Army of Italy was commanded by Napoleon's 28 year old stepson Eugène Beauharnais, who was to cooperate with Général Marmont's XI Corps operating from Dalmatia. Marmont, aged 35, was an artilleryman like Napoleon. To the north-east in Warsaw, Prince Poniatowski, a 46 year old Austrian by birth, was reorganizing the Polish troops of the Duchy of Warsaw to oppose any Austrian aggression in the area.

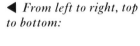

◀ From left to right, top to bottom:

Maréchal Louis-Alexandre Berthier, Prince de Neuchâtel. Aged 56 in 1808, Berthier was now Napoleon's chief of staff. He had first served under Napoleon in 1796 and continued to do so until 1814. At the outbreak of war Berthier was in overall command of the army in Germany. His muddled handling of the early stages almost proved disastrous, but even so at the end of the war he was awarded the title Prince de Wagram. (Hindford Picture Library).

Général Nicolas Charles Oudinot was placed in temporary command of II Corps at the outbreak of war. He had joined the army in 1784 and earned himself the reputation of being a solid fighter, always in the thick of the action, suffering many wounds in the process. Following the Battle of Wagram, where he returned to the command of II Corps, Oudinot was awarded his marshal's baton. (Hindford Picture Library).

Maréchal Jean Lannes, Duc de Montebello. With war imminent in Germany, Lannes was ordered to the new front from Spain to assume command of II Corps from Oudinot. Lannes had joined the army in 1792 and had quickly earned Napoleon's respect as a brave soldier and also as a friend. He was present at most of the main battles of this period and was held in the highest esteem by those who served under him. (Hindford Picture Library).

Maréchal Louis Nicholas Davout, Duc d'Auerstadt, had joined the army in 1788, and found himself in the front line at the outbreak of the 1809 campaign, commanding the experienced III Corps. Having first come to Napoleon's attention in 1798, he performed with distinction at Austerlitz, Auerstadt and Eylau. Although a strict disciplinarian, he was considered one of the ablest marshals. At the close of the campaign he was made Prince d'Eckmuhl. (Hindford Picture Library).

Left: Maréchal André Massena, Duc de Rivoli. The commander of IV Corps had joined the army in 1775 and had experienced a very active military career. He was regarded as a talented leader of men, able to display both cunning and boldness. His great penchant for women and the spoils of war, both of which he freely collected, was widely known. Massena was created Prince d'Essling at the close of the 1809 campaign. (Hindford Picture Library).

Right: Maréchal Jean-Baptiste Jules Bernadotte, Prince de Ponte Corvo. Appointed to command Saxon IX Corps in 1809, Bernadotte voiced his objection to the role, having a low opinion of the troops placed under his command; he later warmed to the task. He had joined the army in 1780 and had seen much action, distinguishing himself in 1805, but he had made a number of enemies amongst fellow senior officers; Napoleon had at times viewed him with suspicion. (Hindford Picture Library).

◀ *Austrian troops, c.1809. To increase the attractiveness of service, the daunting prospect of 25 years enlistment was reduced to ten years in the infantry, twelve in the cavalry and fourteen in the artillery and technical services. New regulations were introduced for the cavalry (1806) and infantry (1807) to break from the old systems in operation since 1769.*

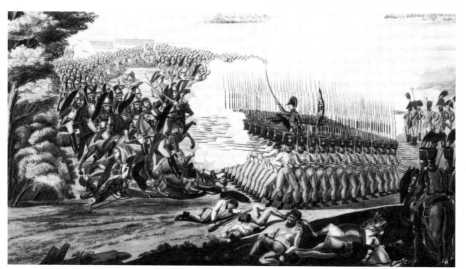

◀ *The favoured Austrian battlefield tactic of the battalion mass proved highly successful during the 1809 campaign. The illustration shows Hungarian infantry in this formation, supported by cavalry and artillery, repelling an attack by cuirassiers. This formation, one company wide and six companies deep, could manoeuvre in open order with gaps between companies which could be rapidly closed. (Anne S. K. Brown Collection).*

OPPOSING ARMIES

The Austrian Army

The Habsburg Army of the Napoleonic period was a vast multi-national entity, its component parts representative of the population of the whole of central Europe. Conditions for these soldiers had improved greatly following Charles' appointment as Generalissimus in 1806, as his reform programme began to take effect and new regulations began to be introduced for all branches of the army.

In 1809 the mainstay of the army was its 46 German and 15 Hungarian line regiments. Each regiment was formed of three battalions, the basic battlefield formation, each of six companies. Company strength was laid down at 218 men for the German units and 238 for the Hungarians, but these figures were rarely attained in the field. Every regiment also had two grenadier companies, each about 145 strong, which were detached on campaign and amalgamated into mixed grenadier battalions of six companies, the élite of the army. The infantry were mostly armed with the 1798 pattern flintlock musket, 150cm long, weighing 4.8kg with a calibre of 17.56mm. When fighting, the infantry formed in three ranks, all standing, although the third rank did not fire. The favoured formation on the battlefield was the battalion mass, devised as an improvement on the square; this was a solid block of men, one company wide by six companies deep. Although vulnerable to artillery fire, this formation could manoeuvre and yet, when closed up, be strong enough to repel cavalry.

In addition to the line regiments, the army also contained nine battalions of Jäger and seventeen

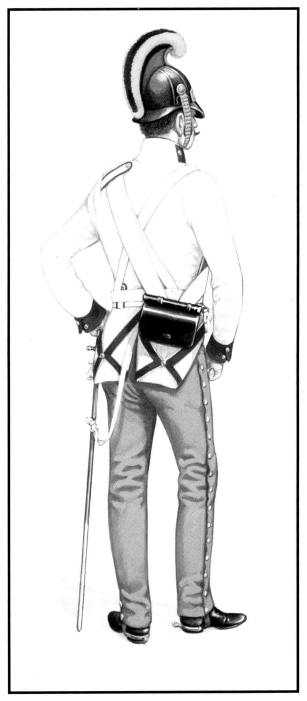

▶ *Austrian trooper of the Herzog Albert cuirassiers. At Wagram this unit clashed with the Saxon Herzog Albert Chevaux-legers, which shared the same Inhaber. The lack of backplate was a serious disadvantage for Austrian cuirassiers when they clashed with their French counterparts. (Bryan Fosten)*

ORDER OF BATTLE: AUSTRIAN ARMY AT THE BATTLE OF ASPERN–ESSLING

Generalissimus: Feldmarschall Erzherzog Karl.

Total strength approx. 99,000 men and 292 guns (excluding artillery crews, engineers, etc.) The numbers of battalions/squadrons and men are given in parentheses.

1ST COLUMN (VI KORPS)
FML Hiller
(Approx. 10,500 infantry, 1,800 cavalry, 52 guns)
Advance Guard Division (GM Nordmann)
7 Liechtenstein Hussars (7; 640 men), IR60 Gyulai (2; 1,717 men); 6 St. Georger Grenzer (1; 686 men); 7 Broder Grenzer (140 men); 1 (544 men) & 2 (610 men) Vienna Volunteers (2)
Division FML Kottulinsky
1 Erzherzog Johann Dragoons (6; 700 men); (GM Hohenfeld) IR14 Klebek (2; 824 men), IR59 Jordis (2; 973 men), 4 Vienna Volunteers (1; 269 men)
Division FML Vincent
(GM Mesko) 8 Kienmayer Hussars (7; 434 men); (Oberst Splényi) IR31 Benjowsky (3; 1,130 men), IR51 Splényi (2; 938 men), 3 Moravian Volunteers (1; 1,057 men); (GM Bianchi) IR39 Duka (2; 1,065 men), 3 Vienna Volunteers (1; 547 men)

2ND COLUMN (I KORPS)
GdK Bellegarde
(Approx. 21,800 infantry, 1,520 Cavalry, 68 guns)
Division FML Fresnel
(GM Vecsey) 4 Vincent (8; 746 men) & 5 Klenau (8; 780 men) Chevauxlegers; (GM Wintzingerode) 2 Jäger (1; 891 men), IR10 Anton Mittrowsky (2; 2,185 men)
Division FML Vogelsang
(GM Henneberg) IR17 Reuss-Plauen (3; 3,313 men), IR36 Kolowrat (3; 3,185 men)
Division FML Ulm
(GM Wacquant) IR11 Erzherzog Rainer (3; 3,254 men), IR47 Vogelsang (3; 3,202 men)
Division FML Nostitz
(Oberst Scharffer) IR35 Argenteau (3; 3,397 men), IR42 Erbach (2; 2,315 men)

3RD COLUMN (II KORPS)
FML Hohenzollern-Hechingen
(Approx. 19,300 infantry, 670 cavalry, 62 guns)
Advance Guard Division
(GM Provenchères) 3 O'Reilly Chevauxlegers (5; 670 men); (GM Mayer) 7 (1; 493 men) & 8 (1; 620 men) Jäger, IR50 Stain (2; 1,062 men), 2 Erzherzog Karl Legion (1; 958 men)
Division FML Brady
(GM Buresch) IR15 Zach (2; 1,548 men), IR57 Josef Collorado (2; 2,064 men); (GM Koller) IR25 Zedtwitz (3; 1,967 men), IR54 Froon (2; 1,500 men)
Division FML Weber
(GM Wied-Runkel) IR18 Stuart (3; 2,937 men), IR21 Rohan (3; 2,874 men), IR28 Frelich (3; 3,305 men)

4TH COLUMN (PART IV KORPS)
FML DEDOVICH (FML ROSENBERG)
(Approx. 11,500 infantry, 2,000 cavalry, 34 guns)
Division FML Klenau (Advance Guard)
(Oberst Hardegg) 2 Schwarzenberg Uhlans (7; 917 men), 1 Jäger (1; 770 men); (Oberst Frelich) 10 Stipsicz Hussars (8; 861 men), IR3 Erzherzog Karl (3; 1,330 men)
Division FML Dedovich
(Oberst Gratze) 2 Moravian Volunteers (1; 993 men), 13 Wallachisch-Illyrisches Grenzer (1; 650 men); (GM Grill) IR8 Erzherzog Ludwig (3; 2,498 men), IR22 Koburg (3; 2,368 men); (GM Neustädter) IR9 Czartoryski (3; 2,248 men), IR55 Reuss-Greitz (2; 692 men), 6 Rosenberg Chevauxlegers (4; 275 men)

5TH COLUMN (PART IV KORPS)
FML Hohenlohe (FML Rosenberg)
(Approx. 10,800 infantry, 1,200 cavalry, 34 guns)
Division FML Rohan (Advance Guard)
(GM Carneville) Carneville Freikorps (208 infantrymen, 115 cavalrymen), 13 Walachisch-Illyrier Grenzer (1; 650 men); (GM Stutterheim) 3 Erzherzog Ferdinand Hussars (8; 821 men), 6 Rosenberg Chevauxlegers (4; 275 men)
Division FML Hohenloe
(GM Riese) IR44 Bellegarde (3; 2,022

men), IR46 Chasteler (3; 1,628 men); (GM Reinhard) IR2 Hiller (3; 3,450 men), IR33 Sztáray (3; 2,871 men)

I RESERVE KORPS
GdK Liechtenstein
Cavalry Reserve
(Approx. 6,670 cavalry, 18 guns)
(GM Wartensleben) 6 Blankenstein Hussars (8; 1,020 men); (GM Kerekes) Primatial Hussars (6; 767 men), Neutraer Hussars (4; 583 men)
Division FML Hessen-Homburg
(GM Siegenthal) 2 Erzherzog Franz (6; 530 men) & 3 Herzog Albert (6; 533 men) Cuirassier; (GM Lederer) 4 Kronprinz Ferdinand (6; 518 men) & 8 Hohenzollern (6; 599 men) Cuirassier
Division FML Kienmayer
(GM Kroyher) 1 Kaiser (4; 290 men) & 6 Liechtenstein (6; 567 men) Cuirassier; (GM Rottermund) 6 Riesch Dragoons (6; 623 men); (GM Clary) 3 Knesevich Dragoons (6; 644 men)
Grenadier Reserve
(Approx. 11,200 infantry, 24 guns)
Division FML Lindenau
(GM Murray) Grenadier battalions, Leiningen (742 men), Portner (713 men), Georgy (745 men), Wieniawsky (837 men), Demontant (778 men), Legraud (744 men), Hohenlohe (708 men), Hahn (523 men)
Division FML d'Aspre
(GM Oberstlt. Scovaud) Grenadier battalions, Brzeczinski (610 men), Puteany (682 men), Scovaud (665 men), Scharlach (706 men), Mayblümel (727 men), Oklopsia (659 men), Bissingen (700 men), Kirchenbetter (613 men)

ORDER OF BATTLE: FRENCH AND ALLIED ARMY AT THE BATTLE OF ASPERN-ESSLING

Emperor Napoleon
Total strength approx. 75,000 men and 152 guns (excl. artillery crews, engineers, etc.)
(*No. of battalions and squadrons given in ())

IMPERIAL GUARD

(Approx. 7,900 infantry, 1,305 cavalry, 8 guns)

1st (Young Guard) Division (GD Curial)
(GB Rouget) Tirailleur chasseurs (2; 1,334 men), Tirailleur grenadiers (2; 1,116 men); (GB Gros) Fusilier chasseurs (2; 1,272 men), Fusilier grenadiers (2; 1,313 men)

2nd (Old Guard) Division (GD Dorsenne)
Chasseurs à pied (2; 1,519 men), Grenadiers à pied (2; 1,324 men),

3rd (Cavalry) Division (GB Arrighi)
(General Guyot) Chasseurs à cheval (2; 363 men), Grenadiers à cheval (1; 219 men), Dragons de l'Imperatice (1; 254 men); (General Krazinski) Chevauxlegers Polonais (2; 414 men), Gendarmerie d'élite (1; 55 men)

II CORPS

Maréchal Lannes
(Approx. 25,600 infantry, 56 guns)

1st Division (GD Tharreau)
(GB Conroux) 4th Batts. of 6e, 24e, 25e Légère (1er Demi-Brigade Légère), and 9e, 16e, 27e Légère (3e Demi-Brigade Légère) (approx. 2,600 men); (GB Albert) 4th Batts. of 8e, 24e, 45e Ligne (1er Demi-Brigade Ligne), and 94e, 95e, 96e Ligne (2e Demi-Brigade Ligne) (approx. 2,600 men); (GB Jarry) 4th Batts. of 54e, 63e Ligne (3e Demi-Brigade Ligne), and 4e, 18e Ligne (4e Demi-Brigade Ligne) (approx. 1,800 men)

2nd Division (GD Claparède)
(GB Coëhorn) 4th Batts. of 17e, 21e, 28e Légère (2e Demi-Brigade Légère), and 26e Légère, Tirailleurs du Po (1), Tirailleurs Corses (1) (4e Demi-Brigade Légère) (approx. 2,300 men); (GB Lesuire) 4th Batts. of 27e, 39e Ligne (5e Demi-Brigade Ligne), 59e, 69e, 76e Ligne (6e Demi-Brigade Ligne) (approx. 1,800 men); (GB Ficatier) 4th Batts. of 40e, 88e Ligne (7e Demi Brigade Ligne), 64e, 100e, 103e Ligne (8e Demi-Brigade Ligne) (approx. 1,700 men)

3rd Division (St. Hilaire)
(GB Marion) 10e Légère (3; approx. 2,060 men); (GB Lorencez) 3e Ligne (3; approx. 1,860 men), 57e Ligne (3; approx. 1,550 men); (GB Destabenrath) 72e Ligne (3; approx. 1,600 men), 105e Ligne (3; approx. 1,400 men)

Reserve Division (GD Demont)
4th Batts. of 7e Légère and 12e, 17e, 21e, 30e, 33e, 61e, 65e, 85e, 111e Ligne (4,264 men)

IV CORPS

Maréchal Massena
(Approx. 27,300 infantry, 4,500 cavalry, 64 guns)

1st Division (GD Legrand)
(GB Ledru) 26e Légère (3), 18e Ligne (3) (combined strength 4,268 men), Baden IR3 Graf Hochberg (2; 1,445 men)

2nd Division (GD Carra St. Cyr)
(GB Cosson) 24e Légère (3); (GB Dalesme) 4e Ligne (3), 46e Ligne (3) (combined strength 7,149 men); Hessen-Darmstadt Brigade; (GM Nagel/GB Schinner) Leib Garde Regiment (2), Leib Regiment (2) (combined strength 2,500 men)

3rd Division (GD Molitor)
(GB Leguay) 2e Ligne (2), 16e Ligne (3); (GB Viviez) 37e Ligne (3), 67e Ligne (2) (combined strength 6,474 men)

4th Division (GD Boudet)
(GB Fririon) 3e Legere (2); (GB Valory) 56e Ligne (3), 93e Ligne (3) (combined strength 5,553 men)

IV Corps Cavalry
(GB Marulaz) 3e, 14e, 19e, 23e Chasseurs à cheval (1,520 men), Baden Leichte Dragoner (4; 260 men), Hessian Garde-Chevauxlegers (3; 150 men), Württemberg Chevauxlegers-Regiment Herzog Heinrich (2; 160 men)

Attached to IV Corps
Light Cavalry Division (GD Lasalle) (GB Bruyère) 13e (3), 24e (3) Chasseurs à cheval (approx. 1,200 men); (GB Piré) 8e Hussars (3), 16e Chasseurs à cheval (3) (approx. 1,240 men)

CAVALRY RESERVE

Maréchal Bessieres
(Approx. 8,400 cavalry (about 5,500 crossed the Danube), 24 guns)

1st Heavy Cavalry Division (GD Nansouty)
(GB Defrance) 1er (4; 551 men) & 2e (4; 585 men) Carabinier; (GB Doumerc) 2e (4; 551 men) & 9e (4; 587 men) Cuirassier; (GB St. Germain) 3e (4; 629 men) & 12e (4; 615 men) Cuirassier

2nd Heavy Cavalry Division (GD St. Sulpice)
(GB Lelièvre de Lagrange) 1er (4; 527 men) & 5e (4; 515 men) Cuirassier; (GB Guiton) 10e (4; 610 men) & 11e (4; 637 men) Cuirassier

3rd Heavy Cavalry Division (GD d'Espagne)
(GB Raynaud) 4e (4; 633 men) & 6e (4; 655 men) Cuirassier; (GB Fouler) 7e (4; 525 men) & 8e (4; 766 men) Cuirassier

---

COMPARATIVE SENIOR MILITARY RANKS

Modern British/US	Austrian	French	Rheinbund
Lieutenant General	Feldzeugmeister (FZM) (Infantry) or General de Kavallerie (GdK) (Cavalry)	–	–
Major General	Feldmarschall-Leutnant (FML)	Général de Division (GD)	General-Leutant (GL)
Brigadier General	General-Major (GM)	Général de Brigade (GB)	General-Major (GM)
Colonel	Oberst	Colonel	Oberst

regiments of Grenz infantry. The Jäger battalions had six companies, each of 166 men when at full strength, and were expected to perform in close order and as skirmishers. The first two ranks of each company were armed with carbines, while the third rank carried rifles. The Grenz (the Military Border between the Habsburg and Ottoman empires) had supplied regiments of tough peasant farmers to the army for more than seventy years. Each Grenz infantry regiment, which were deployed as both line and light infantry, was composed of two battalions of six companies; company strength, set at 220 men, was rarely reached.

The cavalry consisted of 35 regiments, eight cuirassier, six dragoon, six chevauxlegers, twelve hussar and three Uhlan. The heavy cavalry regiments (cuirassiers and dragoons) each fielded six squadrons of about 135 men, the cuirassier having the added protection of a blackened metal breastplate. Both types were armed with a straight sword, cuirassiers additionally carrying a brace of pistols, while the dragoons were issued carbines. The light cavalry (chevauxlegers, hussars and Uhlans) were formed of eight squadrons, each approximately 150 strong. Armament for the chevauxlegers was identical to that of the dragoons; hussars carried a curved sword and carbine, while the Uhlans' main offensive weapon, the lance, was supplemented by a curved sword and a brace of pistols.

Austrian artillery was formed into three types of battery. Brigade Batteries of eight 3pdr or 6pdr guns were allocated to light or line brigades respectively. Cavalry Batteries of four 6pdr and two 7pdr howitzers were allocated to cavalry brigades, and Position Batteries formed the artillery reserve. These batteries were of two types, 6pdr Position (four 6pdr and two 7pdr howitzers) and 12pdr Position (four 12pdr and two 7pdr howitzers), allocated by corps.

Charles had also augmented the regular army by raising the Landwehr, a national militia for the defence of Austrian lands. The planned figure of 180,000 men was not realised for this campaign, but many enrolled enthusiastically as there was much popular support for the war with France. The best of these troops were therefore creamed off and formed into the Volunteer (Freiwilligen) battalions, which joined the main army at the outbreak of war. In Hungary the parliament (Diet) refused to raise a Landwehr but agreed to mobilize the Insurrectio, the cavalry and infantry militia forces of Hungary, Croatia and Slovenia. Like the Landwehr, the troops were of varying quality and inclination.

Just before the outbreak of war, Charles announced a last major reform: the army would adopt a corps system similar to the French. The advantage of the system, amalgamating infantry, cavalry and artillery into self-contained commands, enabled each to fight independently if required and allowed the army to advance on a broader front prior to massing for battle. Charles hoped that the change would enable his army to advance faster than the slow-moving Habsburg armies of the past. Unwilling to follow the French practice of living off the land for fear of provoking local resentment, his much criticized lack of speed in the advance was ultimately dictated by the need to keep in contact with his crawling supply convoys to the rear.

The French Army

When the threat of war became real, many of Napoleon's veterans were embroiled in the cauldron of Spain's bitter war, but the attrition caused by the constant campaigning of the previous years had seen a general lowering of the quality of those in the ranks. In order to boost the available manpower, Napoleon had to dig deep into his reserves; many thousands previously exempt from conscription were called up, and an early enrolment of 30,000 youths from the class of 1810 was found to be necessary.

A reorganization of the line and light infantry regiments (between which there was little tactical distinction) in 1808 gave each regiment four field battalions containing six companies, one of voltigeurs (chasseurs in the light infantry) used for skirmishing, four of fusiliers and one of grenadiers (carabiniers in the light infantry). Large numbers of inexperienced conscripts were required to bring these companies up to their recommended strength of 140 men. Battalions would fire in three ranks, with the front rank kneeling; the voltigeur company would be detached and skirmished in advance of the battalion. The main infantry weapon was the An IX/XIII modification of the 1777 Charleville musket, 151.5cm in length; it weighed 4.375kg and had a calibre of 17.5mm.

To manoeuvre on the battlefield the French preferred the column of divisions, a two company wide formation, three companies deep, while against cavalry the defensive square was favoured. Throughout the campaign of 1809 the infantry was to maintain its tradition of prodigious feats of marching while generally fending for itself.

The cavalry were of two types, heavy and light. All regiments were formed of four squadrons, each of 250 men at full strength, lining up two ranks deep. The heavy cavalry, cuirassiers, carabiniers and dragoons were the strike force; cuirassiers were protected by metal breast- and backplates and were armed with a straight sword and brace of pistols. The carabiniers and dragoons carried similar weapons with the addition of a short musket. The light cavalry, chasseurs à cheval and hussars, the eyes of the army, were armed with curved sabres and a musketoons.

The artillery was in the process of replacing its 4pdr and 8pdr batteries with 6pdrs. As this reorganization was not complete in 1809, all three types were in use during the campaign. Foot batteries were formed of six guns and two howitzers, while horse artillery had only four guns and two howitzers. The Artillery Reserve controlled the powerful 12pdr batteries, which also had howitzer support. Batteries were allocated to each division, a combination of foot and horse artillery to the infantry divisions and horse artillery only to the cavalry divisions.

The shortage of French soldiers because of the commitment in Spain necessitated Napoleon's relying heavily on his German allies in the forthcoming campaign. Having dismantled the Holy Roman Empire, Napoleon reunited the German states under French protection as the

Confederation of the Rhine (Rheinbund). In the early spring of 1809 when the drums of war began to sound, 77,000 Rheinbund soldiers were taking their place in the front line, with a further 25,000 to the rear. The sizes of these contingents varied greatly, from the 30,000 strong Bavarian VII Corps to the composite regiments formed by tiny duchies amalgamating their limited manpower. The

▶ *French trooper of the 5ème Cuirassiers which formed part of the 2nd Heavy Cavalry Division at both Aspern and Wagram. (Angus McBride)*

majority of these contingents readily accepted the new French military doctrines, reforming their forces along French lines, the exception being the Saxons, who made little attempt to modernize their army.

The final piece of Napoleon's military jigsaw to be put into place was the Imperial Guard. Although rarely called upon to provide the telling blow in battle, the Guard was revered for its effect on the morale of the enemy as well as on its own army. Orders were issued for the two regiments of the Old Guard, chasseurs à pied and grenadiers à pied, to be transported from Spain as quickly as possible, while the newly created Young Guard, containing many of the new conscripts, also moved to join the main army. The four regiments of the Young Guard, tirailleur chasseurs, tirailleur grenadiers, fusilier chasseurs and fusilier grenadiers, were each formed into two battalions, all Guard battalions being of four companies, each of about 125 effectives. The Guard Cavalry, with its four élite regiments as well as two squadrons of gendarmes d'élite and one of Mamelukes, headed for the new front; behind them advanced the 60 guns of the Guard Artillery.

As these two huge, similarly equipped armies enlisted and trained their men, Archduke Charles received final confirmation of the decision for war on 8 February 1809. The Austrian Army was placed on a war footing; the plans of campaign debated and finally approved.

ORDER OF BATTLE AUSTRIAN ARMY AT THE BATTLE OF WAGRAM

Generalissimus: Feldmarschall Erzherzog Karl
Total strength approx. 137,700 men and 414 guns (incl. approx. 9,600 artillery, engineers etc.) The numbers of battalions/squadrons and men are given in parentheses.

ADVANCE GUARD
FML Nordmann
(Approx. 11,500 infantry, 2,500 cavalry, 48 guns)
(GM P. Vecsey) Primatial Hussars (6; 756 men), 1 Jäger (1; 526 men), IR58 Beaulieu (2; 1,022 men), 3 Lower Manharts-Berg Landwehr (1; 367 men); (GM Fröhlich) 10 Stipsicz Hussars (8; 968 men), 13 Wallaschisch-Illyrisches Grenzer (2; 1,076 men), 7 Jäger (1; 510 men); (GM Riese) IR44 Bellegarde (3; 1,640 men), IR46 Chasteler (3; 1,601 men), 1 (342 men) & 2 (352 men) Lower Vienna Woods Landwehr (2); (GM Mayer) IR4 Hoch und Deutschmeister (3; 1,064 men), IR49 Kerpen (3; 2,131 men), 5 (340 men) & 6 (325 men) Lower Vienna Woods Landwehr (2); (GM Schneller) 4 Hessen-Homburg Hussars (8; 804 men)

I KORPS
GdK Bellegarde
(Approx. 21,000 infantry, 800 cavalry, 68 guns)
Division FML Dedovich

(GM Henneberg) IR17 Reuss-Plauen (3; 3,124 men), IR36 Kolowrat (3; 3,147 men); (GM Wacquant) IR11 Erzherzog Rainer (3; 2,916 men), IR47 Vogelsang (3; 2,763 men)
Division FML Fresnel
(GM Clary) IR10 Anton Mittrowsky (2; 1,914 men), IR42 Erbach (2; 2,157 men), 1 Hradischer Landwehr (1; 396 men); (GM Motzen) IR35 Argenteau (3; 2,980 men), 4 Erzherzog Karl Legion (1; 952 men); (GM Stutterheim) 5 Klenau Chevauxlegers (8; 801 men), 2 Jäger (1; 743 men)

II KORPS
FML Hohenzollern-Hechingen
(Approx. 25,400 infantry, 520 cavalry, 68 guns)
(GM Hardegg) 4 Vincent Chevauxlegers (6; 517 men), 8 Jäger (1; 551 men), 2 Erzherzog Karl Legion (1; 961 men)
Division FML Brady
(GM Parr) IR25 Zedtwitz (3; 3,210 men), IR54 Froon (3; 3,106 men), 2 Znaimer (1; 504 men) & 3 Hradischer (1; 538 men) Landwehr; (GM Buresch) IR15 Zach (2; 2,080 men), IR57 Josef Colloredo (3; 3,086 men), 1 (597 men) & 3 (495 men) Brunner Landwehr (2)
Division FML Siegenthal
(GM Altstern) IR21 Rohan (3; 3,390 men); (GM Wied-Runkel) IR18 d'Aspre (3; 3,234 men), IR28 Frelich (3; 3,303 men)

III KORPS
FZM Kolowrat
(Approx. 15,900 infantry, 670 cavalry, 58 guns)
(Oberst Schmuttermayer) 2 Schwarzenberg Uhlans (6; 667 men), Lobkowitz Jäger (1; 723 men)
Division FML St. Julien
(GM Lilienberg) IR1 Kaiser (2; 1,489 men), IR12 Manfredini (3; 2,231 men), IR23 Wurzburg (2; 1,419 men); (GM Bieber) IR20 Kaunitz (3; 2,074 men), IR38 Württemberg (2; 1,150 men)
Division FML Vukassovich
(GM Grill) IR7 Carl Schroder (3; 3,174 men), IR56 Wenzel Colloredo (3; 2,562 men); (Oberst Wratislaw) Prague Landwehr (1; 381 men), 1 (349 men) & 2 (377 men) Berauner Landwehr (2)

IV KORPS
FML Rosenberg
(Approx. 17,300 infantry, 840 cavalry, 60 guns)
Division FML Radetzky
(GM Provenchères) 3 Erzherzog Ferdinand Hussars (8; 792 men), Watrich Jäger (1 Erzherzog Karl Legion (1; 657 men)), 2 Moravian Volunteers (1; 691 men), Carneville Freikorps (170 infantrymen & 50 cavalrymen); (GM Weiss) IR3 Erzherzog Karl (3; 3,112 men), IR50 Stain (3; 2,104 men), 4 Lower Vienna Woods Landwehr (1; 350 men), 4

ORDER OF BATTLE AUSTRIAN ARMY AT THE BATTLE OF WAGRAM continued

Upper Manharts-Berg Landwehr (1; 411 men)

Division FML Hohenlohe-Bartenstein
(GM Hessen-Homburg) IR2 Hiller (3; 2,281 men), IR33 Sztáray (3; 2,198 men)

Division FML Rohan
(GM Swinburn) IR8 Erzherzog Ludwig (3; 2,205 men), IR22 Koburg (3; 2,153 men), 1 Iglauer (472 men) & 1 Znaimer (538 men) Landwehr (2)

VI KORPS
FML Klenau
(Approx. 12,500 infantry, 1,275 cavalry, 64 guns)

Division FML Vincent
(GM Wallmoden) 7 Liechtenstein (8; 712 men) & 8 Keinmayer (8; 563 men) Hussars; (GM Mariássy) 1 (508 men) & 2 (582 men) Vienna Volunteers (2), 4 Lower Manharts-Berg Landwehr (1; 690 men); (GM A Vecsey) 6 St. Georger Grenzer (1; 515 men), 7 Broder Grenzer (180 men)

Division FML Hohenfeld
(GM Adler) IR14 Klebek (2; 1,036 men), IR59 Jordis (2; 1,047 men), 3

Erzherzog Karl Legion (1; 518 men), 1 Upper Vienna Woods Landwehr (1; 344 men), Upper Austria Landwehr (1; 771 men); (GM Hoffmeister) IR39 Duka (3; 1,608 men), IR60 Gyulai (3; 1,526 men)

Division FML Kottulinsky
(GM Splényi) IR31 Benjowsky (2; 1,072 men), IR51 Splényi (3; 1,025 men), 3 (463 men) & 4 (330 men) Vienna Volunteers (2), 3 Moravian Volunteers (1; 252 men)

RESERVE KORPS
GdK Liechtenstein
(Approx. 9,900 infantry, 8,050 cavalry, 48 guns)

Grenadier Reserve
Division FML d'Aspre
(GM Merville) Grenadier Battalions, Scharlach, Scovaud, Jambline, Brzeczinski (approx. 1,800 men); (GM Hammer) Grenadier Battalions, Kirchenbetter, Bissingen, Oklopsia, Locher, and 1 Upper Manharts-Berg Landwehr (1) (approx. 2,160 men)

Division FML Prochaska
(GM Murray)
Grenadier Battalions, Frisch, Georgy,

Portner, Leiningen (approx. 2,700 men); (GM Steyrer) Grenadier Battalions, Hahn, Hromada, Legrand, Demontant, Berger (approx. 3,240 men)

Cavalry Reserve
Division FML Hessen-Homburg
(GM Roussel) 2 Erzherzog Franz (6; 480 men) & 3 Herzog Albert (6; 540 men) Cuirassier; (GM Lederer) 4 Kronprinz Ferdinand (6; 540 men) & 8 Hohenzollern (6; 614 men) Cuirassier; (GM Kroyher) 1 Kaiser (4; 420 men) & 6 Moritz Liechtenstein (6; 540 men) Cuirassier.

Division FML Schwarzenberg
(GM Teimern) 3 Knesevich Dragoons (6; 480 men) & 6 Rosenberg Chevauxlegers (8; 720 men); (GM Kerekes) Neutraer Hussars (6; 600 men)

Division FML Nostitz
(GM Rothkirch) 1 Erzherzog Johann (6; 720 men) & 6 Riesch (6; 600 men) Dragoons; (GM Wartensleben) 3 O'Reilly Chevauxlegers (8; 840 men) & 6 Blankenstein Hussars (10; 960 men)

126 ELEMENTS.
19 GUNS.
(16 CAV. / 5 L.I)

▶ *The French army of 1809 was also experiencing a period of change. In 1808 the infantry regiments had been reorganized, giving each regiment four field battalions of six companies each. To bring the regiments up to full strength, large numbers of inexperienced conscripts were needed to bolster the ranks, these being supplied by previously exempt classes and the early enrolment of thousands of youths from the 1810 conscription class. This eroding of the quality of the French infantry, brought about by years of war, manifested itself on a number of occasions during the 1809 campaign. (Anne S. K. Brown Collection).*

ORDER OF BATTLE: FRENCH AND ALLIED ARMY AT THE BATTLE OF WAGRAM

Emperor Napoleon

Total strength approx. 190,500 men and 617 guns (incl. approx. 13,500 artillery, engineers etc.)

IMPERIAL GUARD

(Approx. 7,350 infantry, 3,350 cavalry, 60 guns)

1st (Young Guard) Division (GD Curial)

(GB Rouget) Tirailleur chasseur (2; 1,400 men), Tirailleur grenadier (2; 1,041 men); (GB Dumoustier) Fusilier chasseur (2; 1,089 men), Fusilier grenadier (2; 1,064 men)

2nd (Old Guard) Division

(GD Dorsenne) Chasseurs à pied (2; 1,507 men), Grenadiers à pied (2; 1,250 men)

3rd (Cavalry) Division (GD Walther)

Grenadiers à cheval (4; 699 men), Chasseurs à cheval (4; 1,109 men), Chevauxlegers Polanais (4; 606 men), Dragons de l'Imperatice (4; 718 men), Gendarmerie d'élite (2; 234 men)

II CORPS

GD Oudinot

(Approx. 26,000 infantry, 1,650 cavalry, 64 guns)

1st Division (GD Tharreau)

(GB Conroux) 1er Demi-Brigade Légère (1,377 men) as at Aspern, 3e Demi-Brigade Légère (2,115 men), now formed of 4th Batts. of 9e, 27e Légère and Tirailleurs Corses; (GB Albert) 1er Demi-Brigade Ligne (1,247 men) as at Aspern, 2e Demi-Brigade Ligne (1,526 men) as at Aspern; (GB Jarry) 3e Demi-Brigade Ligne (852 men) as at Aspern, 4e Demi-Brigade Ligne (965 men) as at Aspern

2nd Division (GD Frère)

(GB Coëhorn) 2e Demi-Brigade Légère (1,829 men) as at Aspern, 4e Demi-Brigade Légère (1,628 men), now formed of 4th Batts. of 16e, 26e Légère and Tirailleurs du Po; (GB Razoût) 5e Demi-Brigade Ligne (842 men) as at Aspern, 6e Demi-Brigade Ligne (1,515 men) as at Aspern; (GB Ficatier) 7e Demi-Brigade Ligne (905 men) as at Aspern, 8e Demi-Brigade Ligne (2,056 men) as at Aspern

3rd Division (GD Grandjean)

(GB Marion) 10e Légère (3; 1504 men); (GB Lorencez) 3e Ligne (2,210 men), 57e Ligne (1,838 men); (GB Brun) 72e Ligne (948 men), 105e Ligne (1,183 men)

Portuguese Legion

(GB Carcomelego) 13e Demi-Brigade Élite (3; 1,471 men), Chasseur à Cheval (2; 133 men)

Light Cavalry Brigade

(GB Colbert) 7e (4; 478 men) and 20e (3; 462 men) Chasseurs à Cheval, 9e Hussars (4; 576 men)

III CORPS

Maréchal Davout

(Approx. 31,600 infantry, 6,200 cavalry, 120 guns)

1st Division (GD Morand)

(GB Lacour) 13e Légère (3; 2,012 men), 17e Ligne (3; 2,145 men); (GB l'Huillier) 30e Ligne (3; 2,140 men), 61e Ligne (3; 1,978 men)

2nd Division (GD Friant)

(GB Gilly) 15e Légère (3; 2,013 men), 33e Ligne (3; 2,086 men); (GB Barbanègre) 48e Ligne (3; 1,889 men); (GB Grandeau) 108e Ligne (3; 1,724 men), 111e Ligne (3; 2,079 men)

3rd Division (GD Gudin)

(GB Leclerc) 7e Légère (3; 2,384 men); (GB Boyer) 12e Ligne (3; 1,922 men), 21e Ligne (3; 1,823 men); (GB Duppelin) 25e Ligne (3; 1,447 men), 85e Ligne (3; 1,972 men)

4th Division (GD Puthod)

(GB Girard-vieux) 4th Batts. of 17e Légère, 30e, 33e, 61e, 65e Ligne (1,862 men); (GB Dessailly) 4th Batts. of 7e Légère, 12e, 25e, 85e, 111e Ligne (2,138 men)

Light Cavalry Division (GD Montbrun)

(GB Pajol) 5e Hussars (3; 681 men), 11e (4; 691 men) & 12e (3; 718 men) Chasseurs à cheval; (GB Jacquinot) 7e Hussars (3; 491 men), 1er (4; 351 men) & 2e (3; 377 men) Chasseurs à cheval.

Attached to III Corps

Dragoon Division (GD Pully)

(GB Poinçot) 23e (4; 403 men), 28e (3; 255 men), 29e (4; 451 men) Dragoons

Dragoon Division (GD Grouchy)

(GB Guérin) 7e (4; 492 men), 30e (4; 711 men) Dragoons, Italian Dragoons de la Reine (4; 546 men)

IV CORPS Maréchal Massena

(Approx. 25,100 infantry, 3,000 cavalry, 86 guns)

1st Division (GD Legrand)

(GB Ledru) 26e Légère (3; 1,367 men), 18e Ligne (3; 1,574 men); (Baden Brigade: Oberst Neuenstein) Leib IR1 Grossherzog (2; approx. 1,240 men), IR2 Erbgrossherzog (2; approx. 1,240 men), IR3 Graf Hochberg (2; 1,337 men), Jägerbataillon von Lingg (1; ? men).

2nd Division (GD Carra St. Cyr)

(GB Cosson) 24e Légère (3; 1,738 men); (GB Stabenrath) 4e Ligne (3; 1,963 men), 46e Ligne (3; 1,820 men); Hessen-Darmstadt Brigade (GM Nagel/GB Schinner) Leib Garde Brigade (3; 2,203 men), Leib Brigade (3; 2,149 men)

3rd Division (GD Molitor)

(GB Leguay) 2e Ligne (1,171 men) & 16e Ligne (1,349 men); (GB Viviez) 37e Ligne (1,340 men) & 67e Ligne (885 men)

4th Division (GD Boudet)

(GB Grillot) 3e Ligne (1,270 men); (GB Valory) 56e Ligne (3; 1,307 men), 93e Ligne (2; 1,148 men)

Light Cavalry Brigade

(GB Marulaz) Same as at Aspern minus Württemberg Chevauxlegers (total strength approx. 1,400 men)

Attached to IV Corps

Light Cavalry Division (GD Lasalle)

(GB Bruyère) 13e (493 men), 24e (287 men) Chasseurs à Cheval; (GB Piré) 8e Hussar (449 men) & 16e Chasseurs à Cheval (400 men)

ARMY OF ITALY

Viceroy Eugène
(Approx. 19,600 infantry, 1,800 cavalry, 44 guns)

V CORPS

(GD Macdonald)
1st Division (GD Broussier)
(GB Quétard) 9e Ligne (3; 1,020 men), 84e Ligne (3; 1,020 men); (GB Dessaix) 92e Ligne (4; 1,360 men)
2nd Division (GD Lamarque)
(GB Huart) 18e Légère (2; 680 men), 13e Ligne (3; 1,020 men); (GB Almeiras) 23e Ligne (2; 680 men), 29e Ligne (4; 1,360 men)

VI CORPS

(GD Grenier)
1st Division (GD Seras)
(GB Moreau) 35e Ligne (1; 340 men), 53e Ligne (4; 1,360 men); (GB Roussel) 42e Ligne (1; 340 men), 106e Ligne (3; 1,020 men)
2nd Division (GD Durette)
(GB Valentin) 23e Légère (4; 1,360 men), 60e Ligne (2; 680 men); (GB Bruch) 62e Ligne (3; 1,020 men), 102e Ligne (3; 1,020 men)
3rd Division (GD Pacthod)
(GB Teste) 8e Légère (2; 680 men), 1er Ligne (4; 1,360 men); (GB Abbe) 52e Ligne (4; 1,360 men), 112e Ligne (2; 680 men)
Italian Guard Division (GD Fontanelli)
(GB Guerin) Guard d'Honneur (1; 108 men), Guard Dragoons (2; 248 men); (GB Lecchi) Guard Grenadier (1; 343 men), Guard Chasseur (1; 349 men), Guard Velites (1; 610 men)
Cavalry Division (GD Sahuc)
(GB Gérard) 6e (4; 470 men), 8e (4; 609 men), 9e (3; 409 men) Chasseurs à Cheval

VII CORPS

2nd Bavarian Division (GL Wrede)
(Approx. 5,500 infantry, 1,100 Cavalry, 24 guns)
(GM Minucci) IR3 Prinz Karl (2; 1,442 men), IR13 (2; 1,122 men), 6 leichte bataillon La Roche (1; 542 men); (GM Beckers) IR6 Herzog Wilhelm (2;

1,016 men), IR7 Löwenstein (2; 1,322 men); (Cavalry Brigade GM Preysing) 2 Chevauxlegers König (4; 595 men), 3 Chevauxlegers Leiningen (4; 529 men)

SAXON ARMY

IX CORPS

Maréchal Bernadotte
(Approx. 15,500 infantry, 2,500 cavalry, 38 guns)
1st Division (GL Zezschwitz)
(GM Hartitzsch) Leib Grenadier Garde (1; 511 men), Grenadier Bataillon von Bose (1; 529 men), Grenadier Bataillon von Hake (1; 435 men), Schützen Bataillon von Egidy (1; 474 men); (GM Zeschau) IR König (1; 1,018 men), IR von Niesemeuschel (1; 994 men), IR von Dyherrn & IR von Öbschelwitz (1) (combined, 895 men); (Cavalry Brigade GM Gutschmidt) Garde du Corps (2; 298 men), Carabinier Regiment (2; 209 men), Prinz Clemens Chevauxlegers (4; 418 men), Herzog Albrecht Chevauxlegers (1; 142 men), Hussar Regiment (3; 279 men)
2nd Division (GL Polenz)
(GM Lecoq) IR Prinz Clemens (1; 741 men), IR von Low (1; 946 men), IR von Cerrini (1; 983 men); (GM Steindal) IR Prinz Anton (1; 994 men), IR Prinz Maximilian (1; 1,013 men), IR Prinz Freidrich August (1; 1,004 men); (Cavalry Brigade GM Feilitzsch) Leib Cuirassier Garde (4; 575 men), Prinz Johann Chevauxlegers (4; 538 men)
French/Saxon Division (GD Dupas)
(GB Gency) 5e Légère (2; 1,385 men); (GB Vaux) 19e Ligne (3; 2,048 men), Grenadier Bataillon von Radeloff (1; 529 men), Grenadier Bataillon von Winkelmann (1; 496 men), Schützen Bataillon von Metzsch (1; 548 men)

ARMY OF DALMATIA

XI CORPS

GD Marmont
(Approx. 9,800 infantry, 280 cavalry, 28 guns)
1st Division (GD Claparède)

(GB Bertrand) 18e Légère (2; 1,017 men), 5e Ligne (2; 1,549 men); (GB Delzons) 79e Ligne (2; 1,469 men), 81e Ligne (2; 1,244 men)
2nd Division (GD Clauzel)
(GB Soyez) 8e Légère (2; 1,245 men), 23e Ligne (2; 1,300 men); (GB Bachelu) 11e Ligne (3; 1,923 men); Cavalry: 24e Chasseurs à Cheval (1; 280 men)

CAVALRY RESERVE

Maréchal Bessières
(Approx. 8,200 cavalry, 24 guns)
1st Heavy Cavalry Division (GD Nansouty)
(GB Defrance) 1er (4; 663 men) & 2e (4; 701 men) Carabiniers; (GB Doumerc) 2e (4; 708 men) & 9e (4; 776 men) Cuirassier; (GB Berckheim) 3e (4; 602 men) & 12e (4; 589 men) Cuirassier
2nd Heavy Cavalry Division (GD St. Germain)
(GB Fiteau) 1er (4; 486 men) & 5e (4; 428 men) Cuirassier; (GB Guiton) 10e (4; 592 men) & 11e (4; 488 men) Cuirassier
3rd Heavy Cavalry Division (GD Arrighi)
(GB Raynaud) 4e (4; 444 men) & 6e (4; 491 men) Cuirassier; (GB Bordesoult) 7e (4; 584 men) & 8e (4; 683 men) Cuirassier.

LOBAU ISLAND GARRISON RESERVE

GD Reynier
(Approx. 8,500 infantry and artillery, 129 guns)

23

OPPOSING PLANS

Austria's Options

Austria's plan of campaign was to launch a major surprise attack into Bavaria with eight of its eleven army corps, throwing the French off balance. To the north-east a single corps would march into Poland and defeat France's allies, while in the south the remaining two corps were to march westwards into northern Italy and tie down as many French troops as possible in this secondary theatre.

Charles had initially supported the idea that the main attack should be a bold thrust into Bavaria from Bohemia, north of the Danube. Accordingly, he instructed his chief of staff, Mayer, to order the concentration of six corps in that region, with two south of the river to operate in a supporting role. The plan found favour with Charles as he anticipated Prussian support and expected Britain to launch a diversionary attack in northern Germany. But as these plans progressed Charles began to entertain doubts about the readiness of his army; and, with the news that the Prussians would not rally to his cause after all, he shifted his support to a second plan that advocated launching the main attack *south* of the Danube. Although this would lead to a slower advance because of the number of rivers to be crossed, in theory it allowed communications to be kept open with the army in Italy and offered protection against a French advance on the city of Vienna. A great debate developed in which Mayer opposed Charles' change of heart – which Charles ended by removing his chief of staff from office and dispatching him to the remote garrison of Brod in the Grenz. Now unopposed, he adopted the second, safer plan. On 13 March the slow and exhausting transfer of four corps to join the two already south of the Danube began, hampered and disrupted by the heavy spring rain that turned the few available roads into rivers of mud.

The French Position

Napoleon, in Spain, became aware of increasing Austrian military activity as the year 1809 opened. Having driven the British into retreat, he left the mopping up to Maréchal Soult and returned to Paris; Soult, however, was defeated at Corunna and failed to prevent the escape of the British army.

Back in Paris, Napoleon studied developments. He had not expected Austria's rising again and recognized that his widely dispersed forces, ordered to concentrate in Germany, would be trailing Aus-

trian preparations for war. In case his appearance at the front accelerated Austrian movement, Napoleon remained in Paris, issuing his orders via Berthier at the front. Having believed erroneously that Austria would not make war, he now convinced himself that his enemy would not be ready to launch an attack before 15 April and relaxed a little, under the impression that Austria's ambassador would be withdrawn from Paris before war was declared. Napoleon was to be wrong on both points. At the end of March, Napoleon advised Berthier to concentrate his forces on the Danube in the Regensburg (Ratisbon) area in anticipation of an Austrian attack after 15 April. In the unlikely event that they should move before that date, he was advised to withdraw towards the River Lech at Donauwörth.

The bad weather that was hampering the Austrian transfer of troops to the south of the Danube now took a hand to affect French preparations.

Berthier, an excellent administrator, was out of his depth as an army commander, and the numerous complex orders being received from Napoleon were stretching him to the limit. Poor visibility, caused by the heavy rain, interrupted the flow of telegraph signals, leading to more confusion as courier-delivered instructions arrived out of sequence, causing Berthier to misinterpret Napoleon's instructions and resulting in Davout's III Corps marching aimlessly back and forth. The whole army, dispersed and confused, looked for guidance that the overworked and much stressed Berthier could not supply. On 14 April, Berthier, unable to shoulder the responsibility any longer, wrote to Napoleon: 'In this position of affairs, I greatly desire the arrival of Your Majesty.' Napoleon was in fact already on his way, stung into action by the startling news that the Austrian Army had crossed into Bavaria on 10 April. War had begun.

◀▶*Left and right: In 1809 the Austrian infantry uniform was undergoing major changes in appearance. In about 1798 a classical style leather helmet (left) was introduced. It had initially been considered that the helmet would last twelve years in service, but by 1806 the expense of replacing helmets as a result of damage, being left on the battlefield, or their owners being made prisoner, etc., was proving excessive. This resulted in the introduction of a black cloth shako (right). To reduce an initial large outlay by the Treasury, the new shako was to be introduced gradually, the fifteen Hungarian regiments being first to receive the new headwear while the German units were encouraged to continue wearing the helmet for as long as possible. It is probable that no German regiments had been issued with shakos by 1809.*

Mid-March to 9 April 1809

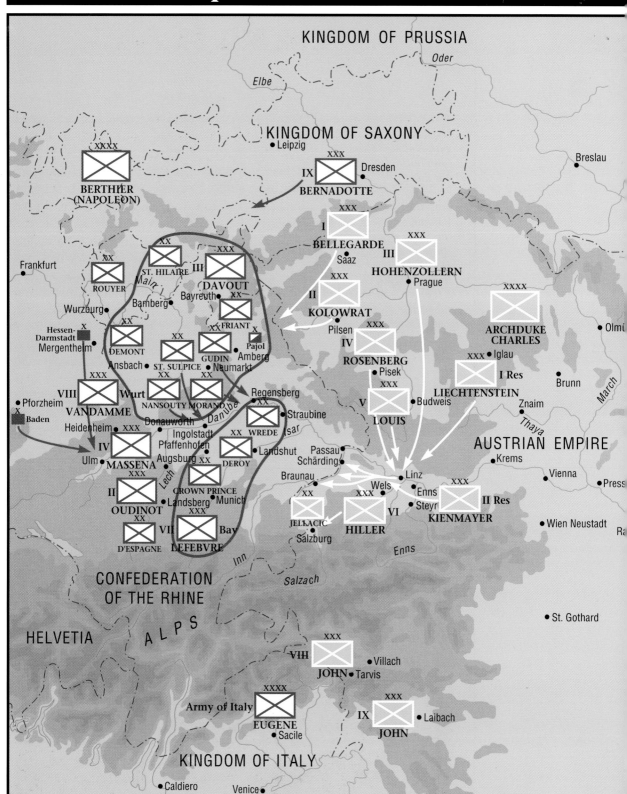

lish/Saxon Army

XXXX Warsaw •
• Raszyn

PONIATOWSKI

XXX Cracow •

VII

FERDINAND

Danube

• Budapest

N

0	25	50 Miles
0	25	50	75	100 Km

OPENING MOVES

▼ *The Battle of Abensberg. On 20 April 1809, with Napoleon now in command, the Bavarians and Württembergers, supported by a provisional corps under Lannes, attacked across the River Abens. The Austrian V Korps and II Reserve Korps were forced to retreat and fell back on Landshut, supported by VI Korps. The illustration shows Bavarian and Württemberg troops leaving the town of Abensberg and advancing towards the Austrian position at Offenstetten, in the distance. (Anne S. K. Brown Collection).*

The main Austrian offensive entered Bavaria across the River Inn at two points. On the right at Schärding, IV Korps (Rosenberg), I Reserve Korps (Liechtenstein) and Vecsey's brigade detached from II Korps pushed over the border; on the left at Braunau, III Korps (Hohenzollern), V Korps (Louis), VI Korps (Hiller) and II Reserve Korps (Kienmayer) similarly moved forward, detaching a division from VI Korps to capture the Bavarian capital of Munich. North of the Danube, I Korps (Bellegarde) and II Korps (Kolowrat) also crossed into Bavaria unopposed, while the secondary theatres were opened in Italy and Poland.

Berthier's muddled handling of the position had ensured that the French and Allied troops were widely dispersed. Davout with III Corps was arrayed in and around Regensburg, while the entire area between the Isar and the Danube was only occupied by the three separated Bavarian divisions of VII Corps (Lefebvre). On the right, far to the

rear, Massena and Oudinot were collecting together IV and II Corps on the River Lech. The Württemberg VIII Corps (Vandamme) was moving on Donauwörth, as were Rouyer's unattached division of Rheinbund troops. Nansouty's heavy cavalry were north of Regensburg, while the Saxons of IX Corps (Bernadotte) and the Imperial Guard were still on their long marches to the centre of operations. In Italy, Eugène and Marmont, and in Poland, Poniatowski, were to oppose the Austrian advances in these areas.

First Contact

The Austrian main army advanced slowly though the rain-soaked countryside, delayed by the weather but meeting no opposition until V Korps (Louis) came into contact with Deroy's Bavarian division, defending the Isar river crossing, at Landshut. A brief engagement ended with the Bavarians withdrawing, aware that further Austrian crossings up- and downstream had outflanked their position. Unaware of Davout's isolated position at Regensburg, Charles intended to push on to the Danube and link with Bellegarde, who was operating north of the river. When he did learn of Davout's predicament, on 18 April, Charles moved forward III Korps (Hohenzollern) and IV Korps (Rosenberg), supported by the grenadiers of I Reserve Korps, to intercept any attempt of the French to debouch from the town, while Liechtenstein led a mixed force directly against it from the south and II Korps (Kolowrat) approached from the north. Archduke Louis' V Korps, supported by II Reserve Korps, was to move towards the River Abens to protect the left of the attacking forces while VI Korps (Hiller) was to shield the left of the whole army.

The Battle Begins

The situation in Bavaria took a dramatic turn with Napoleon's arrival on 17 April; a wave of rekindled enthusiasm flowed through the army as order was restored. Massena's IV Corps and Oudinot's II Corps were directed to move towards Landshut to sever Austrian communications, while Vandamme's VIII Corps began to concentrate around Abensberg, preparing to advance. Davout was ordered to retire

from Regensburg with III Corps and effect a junction with VII and VIII Corps, leaving a small garrison to destroy the stone bridge over the Danube. As Davout marched westwards he encountered elements of the Austrian III and IV Korps. After a bloody struggle on 19 April, principally around the villages of Teugn and Hausen, these formations were unable to halt Davout's progress. With a weakening of the Austrian position, Napoleon launched the Battle of Abensberg.

On 20 April the Bavarians and Württembergers, supported by a provisional corps created for the recently arrived Lannes, crossed the Abens and smashed into V Korps (Louis), forcing it and II Reserve Korps back. Hiller, who had been ordered to close the gap with V Korps, now found himself attempting to delay the oncoming French and Allied troops with his own corps. Meanwhile, Napoleon, believing these three corps to be the Austrian main army, pursued them to Landshut, where they made a stand before being forced to retreat again, disordered but not beaten. At this point, Napoleon realised that Davout, with only III Corps, was now confronting the main body of the Austrian army alone, since the Emperor had ignored his pleas for assistance. Detailing a force to pursue Hiller's three corps, he immediately arranged his troops for a march north to support Davout. This manoeuvre culminated in the victory at Eggmühl on 22 April. Charles retreated to Regensburg, which had been taken from the French garrison with its massive bridge intact, and was able to retire safely to the north bank of the Danube, a great cavalry battle at Alt Egolfsheim gaining time for the manoeuvre. Charles now began his retreat through Bohemia, having witnessed Napoleon's unsurpassed ability for battlefield manoeuvre at first hand. However, like Hiller's force, although his army was disordered it remained intact; Napoleon had failed to destroy any of the Austrian corps. In fact, during the retreat Hiller was able to turn on his pursuers at Neumarkt and inflict a painful reverse before retiring to Ebelsberg, where he made another stand before retiring again and crossing to the north bank of the Danube.

Meanwhile, in Italy and Poland initial Austrian successes had been followed by regrouping and retirement as French and Allied troops recovered and took the initiative.

Vienna Surrenders

Outstripping the retreating Austrians, Napoleon, leaving VII Corps to deal with a growing insurgency in the Tyrol, pushed on to Vienna, protecting his communications along the Danube by detaching first VIII Corps then III Corps as he went. Arriving before the city with II Corps (now assigned to Lannes as originally intended), Massena's IV Corps and cavalry support, he accepted the surrender of Vienna on 13 May following a short bombardment. The occupation of the city was a hollow victory for Napoleon as the Austrian army was still at large and, he believed, marching away to the north. To defeat Austria decisively he knew he would have to cross the Danube and seek fresh confrontation. However, unknown to the French, Charles had arrived on the Marchfeld, a vast flat plain north-east of the city, on 16 May and was reorganizing his army for battle.

Unhappy with the performance of his corps system, Charles now ordered a return to a single army command. An army Advance Guard was created and placed under FML Klenau, and the two Reserve Korps were amalgamated under Liechten-stein, forming the Grenadier Reserve and Cavalry Reserve, to which all corps cavalry would be transferred. During the retreat, III Korps had been detached on the Bohemian frontier to oppose any pursuit, control passing to Kolowrat, while Hohenzollern competed the exchange of commands by assuming control of II Korps. In total, Charles could call on about 110,000 men; Napoleon, who had distributed so many of his men on the line of march, commanded approximately 80,000.

Eager to come to grips with the Austrians and inflict the decisive defeat he knew was necessary, Napoleon ordered a river crossing upstream of Vienna, opposite Nussdorf, as the city's bridges had been destroyed. The French, having gained a foothold on the Schwarzen Lackenau, one of the islands on the Austrian bank, were confronted by stiff resistance and, after suffering heavy casualties, withdrew, leaving the Austrians in possession after six hours' fighting. Archduke Charles later stated that without this French repulse there would have been no battle of Aspern-Essling. Impatient because of the failure to force a passage at this point, Napoleon turned his attention to Lobau island, downstream of Vienna.

▶ *The surrender of Vienna. Following the defeat of the Austrians at Eggmühl, Napoleon pushed on to Vienna largely unopposed. The French reached the suburbs of the city on 10 May. The following evening a bombardment commenced from the Prater, an island in the Danube, and during the early hours of 12 May the Austrians began an evacuation of the majority of the garrison. The surrender of the city took place on 13 May. (Anne S. K. Brown Collection).*

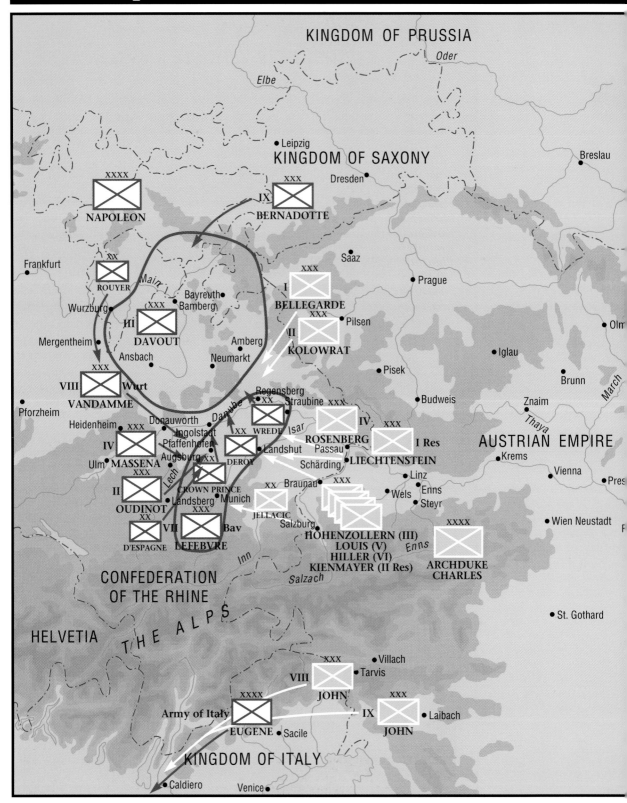

KINGDOM OF PRUSSIA

Oder

Elbe

• Leipzig

KINGDOM OF SAXONY

Dresden •

Breslau

XXXX

NAPOLEON

XXX

IX

BERNADOTTE

Saaz •

• Prague

Frankfurt •

XX

ROUYER

Main

Bayreuth •
Bamberg •

XXX

I

BELLEGARDE

XXX

Pilsen •

Wurzburg •

XXX

HI

DAVOUT

II

KOLOWRAT

Mergentheim •

Amberg •

Ansbach •

Neumarkt •

• Iglau

Brunn

March

Znaim •

XXX

VIII

Wurt

VANDAMME

Regensberg •
XX
Straubine XXX

Danube

• Budweis

Thaya

AUSTRIAN EMPIRE

Pforzheim •

Heidenheim •

XXX

Donauworth

Danube

XX WREDE

Isar

IV

XXX

I Res

Krems •

Ingolstadt
Pfaffenhofen

ROSENBERG
Passau •

Vienna •

Pres

IV

MASSENA

Ulm •

XXX

Augsburg XX

Lech

Landshut

Schärding •

LIECHTENSTEIN

• Linz

• Enns

DEROY

XX

Braunau

XXX

• Wels

Steyr •

II

OUDINOT

XXX

CROWN PRINCE

Landsberg • Munich

XX

JELLACIC

Salzburg •

HOHENZOLLERN (III)

XXXX

• Wien Neustadt

F

VII

XXX

LEFEBVRE

XX

D'ESPAGNE

Bav

LOUIS (V)
HILLER (VI)
KIENMAYER (II Res)

ARCHDUKE
CHARLES

Enns

CONFEDERATION
OF THE RHINE

Inn

Salzach

• St. Gothard

HELVETIA

THE ALPS

XXX

• Villach

VIII

• Tarvis

JOHN

XXXX

XXX

Army of Italy

IX

• Laibach

EUGENE • Sacile

JOHN

KINGDOM OF ITALY

• Caldiero

Venice •

30

THE BATTLE OF ASPERN-ESSLING

XXX Cracow

VII
FERDINAND

▼ *Austrian attempts to disrupt the French river crossing proved highly successful. By sending down the river an endless stream of floating obstacles Napoleon's attempts to reinforce his hard-pressed army were seriously hampered. The illustration shows from left to right, a Pontooner, Pioneer, a Pontooner and Pioneer at work, an officer of the Ingenieurs Corps and a Pioneer officer.*
(Romain Baulesch)

Crossing the Danube

The modern aspect of the Danube at Vienna is very different from that which confronted Napoleon in 1809. In the latter half of the nineteenth century, work was carried out to regulate the river, thus removing the tangle of countless streams, river branches, arms and islands that faced the French as they prepared to cross to the Marchfeld. Lobau island, downstream from Vienna and selected as the French base of operations, was to be linked to the south bank by a single bridge. The first span, 450m long and reaching the Schneidergrund, was followed by a second continuing on to Lobgrund, a further 225m, where it joined Lobau. Paying no heed to the force of the river that was rapidly becoming swollen by the melting mountain snows upstream, Napoleon ordered those troops in the Vienna area to congregate near Kaiser-Ebersdorf prior to crossing. Charles had been made aware of the

anube

• Budapest

N

0   25   50 Miles
0   25   50   75   100 Km

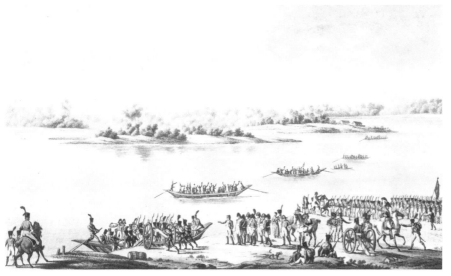

◀ *At about 5.00 p.m. on 18 May Napoleon ordered Molitor to cross the Danube with part of his division and secure the midstream islands in preparation for a bridge to be thrown across. On Lobgrund a little resistance was encountered from Austrian outposts, but on the following day Molitor moved on to Lobau and by 3.00 p.m. the main island was cleared. (Anne S. K. Brown Collection).*

◀ *With Lobgrund declared clear on 18 May, work immediately began on constructing a single bridge of boats, with planks laid over, from the bank of the Danube at Kaiser Ebersdorf. Work continued throughout the next two days until the bridge reached Lobau by midday on 20 May. (F. Wöber).*

◀ *At 3.00 p.m. on 20 May, work started on the final stretch of bridge that would link Lobau with the Mühlau on the left bank of the Danube. Molitor's men opened fire across the Stadtler Arm, driving off the Austrian outposts before 200 voltigeurs crossed by boat to secure the bridgehead as construction continued. (Anne S. K. Brown Collection).*

build-up of French troops and of their bridging operations at Lobau, but it had been decided to allow the French to cross without any serious opposition. It was felt among the Austrian staff that if the French crossed and were beaten they would find themselves in a difficult position with the river at their backs and the additional worry of a potentially hostile population, encouraged by this turn of events, across their communications.

On 19 May the first French troops occupied Lobau, an island about 4 kilometres wide covered in trees and thick bush. The following day 200 voltigeurs rowed 150m across the last branch of the river, the Stadtler Arm, and moved on to the Mühlau, a partially wooded salient, driving off outposts of Klenau's Advance Guard. The build-up of troops on Lobau continued smoothly until about 5.00 p.m. on 20 May, when a stone-filled barge, sent down the flooded river by the Austrians, smashed into the bridge between Schneidergrund and Lobgrund, rendering it non-operational until the following morning. At 6.00 p.m. that evening the final bridge to the Mühlau was in place and the units on Lobau began to cross. First went Molitor's infantry of IV Corps followed by Lasalle's light cavalry division, who pushed Klenau's Advance Guard back farther before Austrian cavalry support arrived and forced Lasalle back to the Mühlau. Molitor's men had meanwhile occupied the villages of Aspern and Essling. Seeking the whereabouts of Charles' army, Napoleon ordered an observation report from the church tower at Aspern. Around midnight Massena observed a number of camp fires around the Bisemberg, a great hill overlooking the Danube north of Vienna – but not nearly enough for the whole army. This intelligence confirmed Napoleon's suspicions that only a rearguard lay before him, the main army moving north. Napoleon was partly right. The Austrians were moving, but not northwards as suspected; they were heading for the French positions at the villages of Aspern and Essling.

At about 3.00 p.m. on 20 May, Charles, informed that the French were about to launch their crossing, ordered his army to their new positions ready to attack. Throughout the night, undetected by French cavalry patrols, the Austrian corps moved into their assigned positions, forming a great, gently curving arc more than 12 kilometres long on the heights bordering the Marchfeld, from Strebersdorf to Deutsch-Wagram.

21 May 1809: The First Day

Whit Sunday, 21 May, dawned hot and still, the sun soon burning off the early morning mist. Austrian attempts to disrupt traffic on the French bridges had continued through the night, but at 8.00 a.m. Massena was able to order Boudet and Legrand's divisions forward from the Mühlau. Having cleared Gross-Enzersdorf of Austrian outposts, Boudet's men relieved the part of Molitor's division that had occupied Essling overnight, allowing them to rejoin the rest of their division at Aspern. Legrand's division was also ordered towards Aspern to provide support for Molitor. Possession of these two villages was to prove of the utmost importance on the otherwise featureless plain.

Aspern was a reasonably prosperous village of 106 brick-built houses, mainly along two roads that ran west to east through the village, connected by cross-streets. The church at the western end, on slightly higher ground, had a cemetery with a chest-high wall as well as a vicarage and garden surrounded by a lower wall. South of the village was a water-filled ditch that flowed around the Gemeinde Au, a heavily overgrown area of trees and bush, and back into the Danube. Other ditches ran to the west of the village, as well as the man-made one on the north side, with its earth bank that carried away flood water when the Danube was high. The earth bank and ditch continued along the side of the road to Essling.

Smaller than Aspern, Essling consisted of 55 houses, either side of the village pond. The most important feature of the village was the huge three-storey granary, with walls a metre thick. West of the granary was the walled Great Garden and on the south side was the Long Garden, surrounded by ditches, ending a short distance from the Stadtler Arm of the Danube.

The Austrian Plan

At 9.00 a.m., with little activity on the Marchfeld, Charles called his corps commanders to his new headquarters at Gerasdorf and informed them of his

Aspern-Essling, 21-22 May 1809; Day One

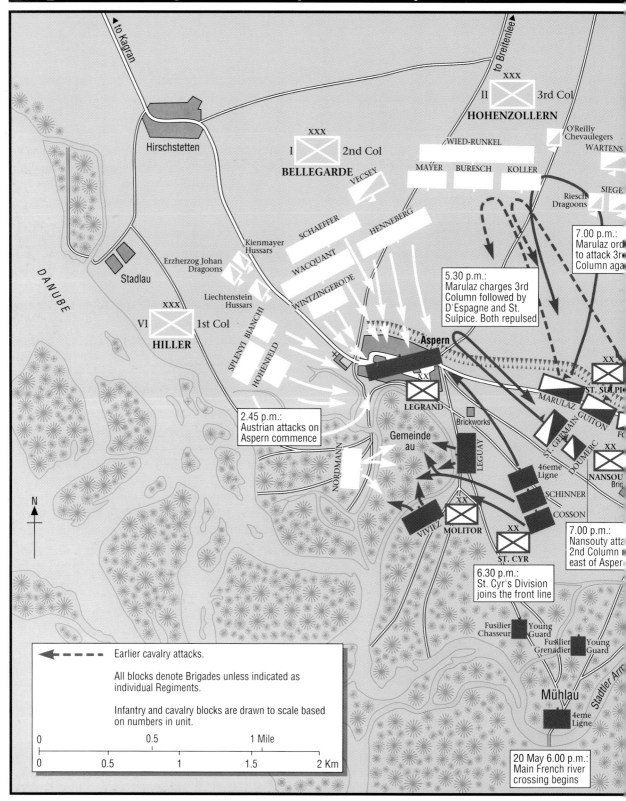

to Kagran

to Breitenlee

Hirschstetten

XXX
II ⊠ 3rd Col
HOHENZOLLERN

O'Reilly
Chevaulegers
WIED-RUNKEL
WARTENS

XXX
I ⊠ 2nd Col
BELLEGARDE

VECSEY

MAYER   BURESCH   KOLLER

SIEGE

Riesch
Dragoons

SCHAEFFER   HENNEBERG

Kienmayer
Hussars

7.00 p.m.:
Marulaz ord
to attack 3r
Column aga

5.30 p.m.:
Marulaz charges 3rd
Column followed by
D'Espagne and St.
Sulpice. Both repulsed

Erzherzog Johan
Dragoons

WACQUANT

Stadlau

Liechtenstein
Hussars

WINTZINGERODE

DANUBE

XXX
VI ⊠ 1st Col
HILLER

SPLENYI BLANCHI

HOHENFELD

Aspern

XX
⊠ ST. SULPI

XX
⊠
LEGRAND

MARULAZ

2.45 p.m.:
Austrian attacks on
Aspern commence

Brickworks

Gemeinde
au

ST. GERMAIN GUITON

XX
⊠
NANSOU
Bri

46eme
Ligne

DOUMERC

NORDMANN

LEGUAY

SCHINNER

COSSON

7.00 p.m.:
Nansouty atta
2nd Column
east of Asper

XX
⊠
VIVIEZ **MOLITOR**

XX
⊠
ST. CYR

6.30 p.m.:
St. Cyr's Division
joins the front line

N

Fusilier
Chasseur

Young
Guard

Fusilier
Grenadier

Young
Guard

Mühlau

Stadtler Ar

⬅ - - - - Earlier cavalry attacks.

All blocks denote Brigades unless indicated as
individual Regiments.

Infantry and cavalry blocks are drawn to scale based
on numbers in unit.

4eme
Ligne

0	0.5	1 Mile

| 0 | 0.5 | 1 | 1.5 | 2 Km |

20 May 6.00 p.m.:
Main French river
crossing begins

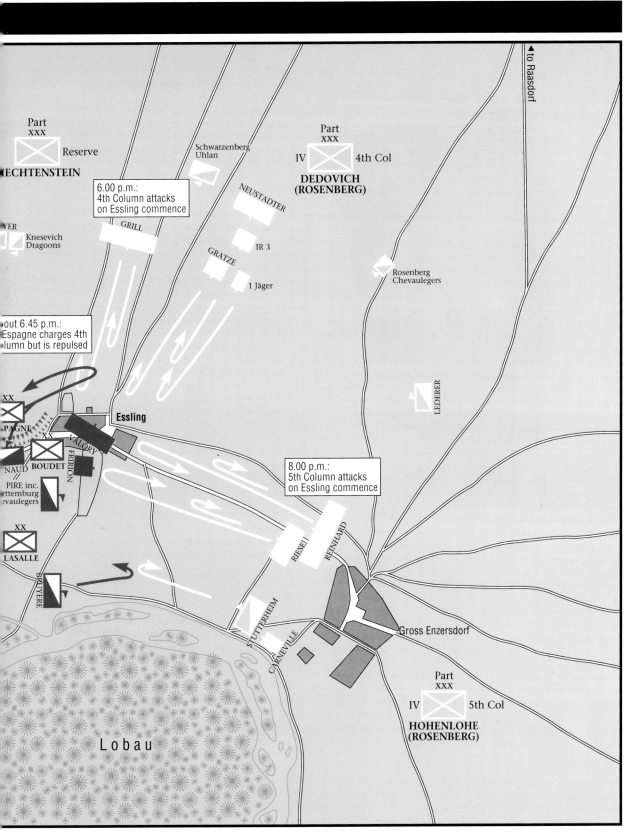

Part
XXX

Reserve

ECHTENSTEIN

YER

Knesevich
Dragoons

Schwarzenberg
Uhlan

NEUSTADTER

GRILL

GRATZE

IR 3

1 Jäger

Part
XXX

IV   4th Col

DEDOVICH
(ROSENBERG)

▲ to Raasdorf

Rosenberg
Chevaulegers

LEDERER

6.00 p.m.:
4th Column attacks
on Essling commence

out 6.45 p.m.:
Espagne charges 4th
lumn but is repulsed

XX

PAGNE

XX

NAUD   BOUDET

VALORY

FRIRON

PIRE inc.
rttemburg
evaulegers

XX

LASALLE

BRUYERE

Essling

8.00 p.m.:
5th Column attacks
on Essling commence

RIESE

REINHARD

STUTTERHEIM

CARNEVILLE

Gross Enzersdorf

Part
XXX

IV   5th Col

HOHENLOHE
(ROSENBERG)

Lobau

◄ The modern church at Aspern, which replaced that destroyed in the fighting of 21/22 May, was built on the site of its predecessor. This area witnessed the bloodiest fighting of the battle. The poignant monument to the battle, which stands in front of the church, represents Austria as a wounded lion, pinning a French eagle beneath its paws.

plan of attack. Charles believed that only a part of Napoleon's army was about to advance, striking towards Hirschstetten to secure the north bank of the river for a second attempted crossing in the Nussdorf area. Charles' plan formed his four infantry corps into five attack columns, with the grenadiers and cavalry in reserve.

The attack was to be led by 1st Column (VI Korps), 2nd Column (I Korps) and 3rd Column (II Korps), converging from starting points on the heights to intercept the anticipated French movement, with 1st Column on the right. To their left, 4th and 5th Columns, formed from IV Korps, were to sweep around towards Essling, turning on the village of Raasdorf and threatening the French rear. The gap that would open between the Columns attacking Aspern and Essling would be filled by Liechtenstein with the Reserve Cavalry, who, if all went according to plan, would find himself in a position to imperil the French right flank. However, the recently strengthened Reserve Cavalry was now weakened again as the Column commanders requested cavalry protection while they prepared to

march on to the exposed expanses of the Marchfeld. The Grenadier Reserve moved forward to Gerasdorf behind the attack columns; V Korps (Louis), which was widely distributed watching the river crossings upstream, remained centred at Strebersdorf and took no part in the coming battle. Before marching off, Charles ordered an address to be read to his army, urging them by their bravery to decide the fate of the monarchy and their own freedom. With cries of 'Long live the Emperor!' and 'Long live Charles!' echoing forth, the white-coated army prepared to advance.

The Battle Begins

As the morning progressed, emergency repairs to the bridge enabled GD d'Espagne to cross with his heavy cavalry division and GB Marulaz with the light cavalry of IV Corps, a mixed French and German force. The crossing had to be carried out slowly and dismounted, as the bridges were in a very frag-

▶ *The heavily wooded Gemeindeau, south of the village of Aspern, was the scene of much confused fighting. This illustration shows a group of Vienna Volunteers, part of Nordmann's Advance Guard of the 1st Column, engaging elements of Massena's IV Corps under the watchful eye of Archduke Charles. (R. Baulesch).*

ile condition – in many places the river actually flowed over the planks. Napoleon was now based at the brick ovens just east of Aspern when at 1.00 p.m. he received news from his outposts that a vast Austrian army was advancing towards him with drums playing and colours held high. Having concentrated on bringing his cavalry over for the pursuit of a *retreating* enemy, he now had only three infantry divisions on the north bank, about 17,000 men, to defend his position. With about 4,500 light cavalry and 2,500 heavy cavalry, he had at the outset 24,000 men and 40 guns against approximately 99,000 Austrians with 292 guns. While he was digesting this news, Napoleon was informed that the bridge had again been broken. With problems to his front and rear, he contemplated withdrawing to Lobau but was persuaded by his subordinates to defend the strong position based on the twin villages. As the sound of gunfire was heard, Napoleon charged Massena with the responsibility of holding Aspern with Molitor's division, supported by Legrand's division positioned south-east of the village, facing the Gemeinde Au. Lannes, whose corps had not been able to cross, took command of Massena's other division, Boudet's, with orders to

defend Essling. The ground between the two villages was to be held by the cavalry under Maréchal Bessières.

The first clashes took place between GM Nordmann's advance guard of 1st Column (VI Korps) and Marulaz's cavalry outposts. The first weak attempt on Aspern failed, but a second by a battalion of IR60 (Gyulai) at 2.45pm briefly entered the village before being easily ejected by Viviez's brigade. Molitor then pushed Leguay's brigade into the village to bolster the defence.

As the Austrians re-formed, the main body of 1st Column moved into position, FML Kottulinsky's division in the first line with FML Vincent's division behind. At the same time, to their left, the 2nd Column (I Korps) also moved into position, detaching Wintzingerode's brigade to support Hiller's next assault that was launched at about 3.30 p.m. Largely uncoordinated, the attack by eight battalions, line infantry, Jäger, Grenzer and Volunteers, from the north, west and south-west, was repelled by the French defenders with huge Austrian losses.

In the distance the Austrian 3rd Column (II Korps) was now moving into position to the left of 2nd Column, its artillery opening fire in support of the attacks on Aspern. Napoleon, now recognizing that the Austrians were converging on him in a great crescent around the two villages, ordered all available artillery to form in the centre to support the weaker position at Essling. Rosenberg's 4th and 5th Columns, commanded by FML Dedovich and

◀ *The granary at Essling as it appears today. This massive stone building has changed little over the intervening 185 years. The village of Essling lies hidden behind the trees to* *its rear. It was across this flat country, devoid of cover, that Austrian troops attempted to storm this French bastion throughout the battle.*

◀ *Control of the village of Aspern changed hands many times during the two days of the battle. In this illustration, Hungarian infantry storm towards the burning church at the western end of the village. Urged forward by mounted officers, the infantry are attacking the high wall that surrounded the church. (Bibliothèque des Arts Decoratifs, Paris, Collection Maciet).*

FML Hohenloe had by far the longest approach marches to reach their assault positions, so for the time being all remained relatively quiet in Essling.

Liechtenstein with the Reserve Cavalry had moved beyond the Breitenlee–Neu Wirsthaus road in the centre, where it came under artillery fire. Having moved GM Kroyer's cuirassier brigade out of range and dispatched two dragoon regiments to oppose a flanking move by some French cavalry, two cuirassier brigades of FML Hessen-Homburg's division were attacked by d'Espagne's heavy cavalry division at

about 3.30 p.m. A slight initial French superiority in numbers was soon negated as the detached Austrian cuirassiers and dragoons were recalled and joined the great swirling mêlée. Now outnumbered, the French held their own until a regiment of Uhlans from 4th Column and hussars from the Reserve tipped the scales and d'Espagne's valiant troopers fell back behind the Aspern-Essling ditch. With a clear field of fire again, the French artillery resumed their attack on the Austrian cavalry from Essling at about 4.00 p.m., forcing the shaken horsemen to retire behind

Hohenzollern's 3rd Column, which had been moving to the left to ease the growing congestion around Aspern. As the cavalry withdrew, 4th Column (half of IV Korps) arrived north of Essling but could not attack until 5th Column (half of IV Korps) had drawn itself up beyond Gross-Enzersdorf.

The Austrians launched another great attack on Aspern at about 4.30 p.m. supported by a storm of shot and shell, the exhausted defenders losing control of the church and cemetery after fierce hand-to-hand fighting. Concerned that the Austrians were getting the upper hand, Napoleon ordered Bessières to attack the artillery and infantry of 3rd Column, which were pouring such destruction into Aspern. Legrand's division was ordered to support Molitor's men in the village. The first unit, 26ème Légère, arriving at about 5.30 p.m., were just in time to halt the Austrian sweep through the streets.

The First Cavalry Attack

In accordance with their orders, Marulaz's cavalry began to advance at about the same time. An attempt by Austrian cavalry to halt the attack failed, but as the light horsemen passed through the Austrian guns they were confronted by infantry drawn up in battalion masses, whose close-range fire against the unsupported light cavalry caused the horsemen to retreat. Bessières then sent d'Espagne's cuirassier division forward, with two regiments from St. Sulpice's division, which had now arrived on the Marchfeld, to attack the solid infantry. At 300 paces the cavalry halted and demanded the Austrians surrender – which was greeted with a discharge of musketry. The cavalry charged, but the masses, with great discipline, held their fire until the enemy were within fifteen paces, when volleys of immense destruction erupted forth; screams of horses and cries of men rent the air as all were engulfed in great clouds of smoke. Those not hit

◄ *German infantry wearing the crested helmet storm towards the main village of Aspern, having gained control of the church, shown in the left background. This illustration depicts the*

Battalion Mass formation in open order, with gaps kept between each of the three rank companies. Should cavalry attack, these gaps would have been closed up. (F. Wöber).

milled impotently around the infantry formations or clashed with the re-forming Austrian cavalry in the rear before retreating back to their starting line close to Essling.

Battle Rages in Aspern

Back in Aspern the timely arrival of the 26ème Légère had balanced the situation again, but when IR17 (Reuss-Plauen) lost three senior officers in quick succession the regiment fell back, taking the other Austrian units with them and returning control of the village once more to the French. Molitor's men, now having suffered about 50% casualties, were relieved and withdrawn from the shattered village to rest, Legrand's 18ème Ligne joining the 26ème Légère, supported by the Baden IR3 (Graf Hochberg).

Before 6.00 p.m. another attempt to retake the village failed in the face of determined French opposition. Archduke Charles, aware of the importance of capturing and holding the village, informed Bellegarde that he must take it at whatever cost. Once more the Austrians flung themselves at the smouldering ruins that had once been the village of Aspern. The attack was led by Wacquant's brigade of six battalions; in support and on each flank were arrayed a further thirteen battalions. With all troops in place, Wacquant took the standard of 1tes Battalion IR47 (Vogelsang) and led his men forward with the cry, 'Long live Emperor Francis! Conquer or die!' Moments later he fell wounded. The advance faltered before the cemetery in the face of murderous French fire, at which point Charles, at great personal risk, rode amongst the men and cried out, 'For the Fatherland! Forward courageously!' Inspired by this brave act, the men stormed forward, retaking church and cemetery. The fighting in the village now took on a new level of ferocity as soldiers of both sides fought for control of every defensible position; every burnt-out building, wall or out-house became a fortress, individuals firing from behind gravestones, dungheaps or anything that offered protection from the enemy. The battle swung one way and then the other until the arrival of Austrian artillery in the village around 6.30 p.m. forced Legrand's men to pull out. Napoleon, almost caught up in the evacuation, immediately ordered its recapture.

◀ Shortly after 6.00 p.m., Charles ordered Bellegarde to retake Aspern 'at whatever cost'. The attack was led by GM Wacquant's brigade of 2nd Column. The illustration shows IR11, which spearheaded the attack with IR47, closing on the smouldering church. For his bravery Wacquant was awarded the Order of Maria Theresa. (Aspern Museum, Vienna).

French efforts to bring men across the Danube had been severely hampered all day by the succession of barges, fire-ships, floating mills and burning rafts that the Austrians had been sending down the river. This tactic had limited French reinforcements to a trickle, but by about 6.30 p.m. St. Cyr's division (about 9,000 men and 18 guns), the missing element of Massena's IV Corps, had managed to cross and (less one regiment) were immediately directed towards Aspern. On arrival, the Hessen-Darmstadt brigade was placed on the wooded Gemeinde Au, the 24ème Légère were aligned with Molitor's men outside the village, and the 46ème Ligne were ordered to retake Aspern. The scattered and disorganized defenders reeled back before this fresh onslaught, but an Austrian counter-charge forced the attackers back to the lower part of the village.

Further reinforcements followed St. Cyr's men across the river. Nansouty crossed with St. Germaine's cuirassier brigade, but as Doumerc's brigade followed the bridge collapsed once more, and a number of the 2nd Cuirassiers were carried away and drowned.

The First Attacks on Essling

Shortly after the French cavalry attacks against the infantry of 3rd Column, the Austrian 4th Column began a series of uncoordinated attacks against Essling. These floundered against the massive stone bastion of the granary, although IR55 (Reuss-Greitz) managed to hold a position in the cemetery on the edge of the village. As the assault column retired, Lannes, in command of the defence, ordered the recently returned cavalry of d'Espagne to pursue them. The infantry reacted by forming battalion masses, which prevented any French success, and the disordered cavalry were then attacked by their Austrian counterparts, resulting in another great cavalry mêlée. D'Espagne was mortally wounded, his men withdrawing after the intervention of Piré's brigade of light cavalry and the Württemberg Herzog Heinrich Chevauxlegers.

Napoleon, observing Liechtenstein now placing his Reserve Cavalry between 3rd and 4th Columns, feared the Austrians were about to launch an attack against his weak centre, which if successful would have jeopardised his whole position. To stave off this attack Napoleon again called on his cavalry, ordering Nansouty to attack the enemy batteries at the north-east edge of Aspern with three cuirassier regiments; he also instructed Marulaz to attack the junction between Hohenzollern's 3rd Column and the Reserve Cavalry. The cuirassiers brushed aside a counter-charge by six squadrons of light cavalry, but the fire of two battalions protecting the guns threw the French into a confusion that was exploited by an opposing cuirassier regiment, which drove them off. Marulaz had hit the Austrian cavalry hard in his attack and broken through the first line before turning into Hohenzollern's infantry. Once more the masses stood up to the cavalry attacks. With artillery and cavalry support, they then forced Marulaz to retire, bringing an end to the action in the centre for that evening.

While the centre was now static, the action flared up in front of 5th Column, which had even-

tually reached a position to attack Essling at about 8.00 p.m. Their first attack was led by four battalions, with two battalions on the left in support and five in reserve. By 9.00 p.m. the houses at the eastern edge of the village had been captured, but the Long Garden was held only briefly. The continuing uncoordinated nature of attacks on Essling allowed Lannes to deploy his outnumbered men at the critical point each time to maintain control of the village. At 9.30 p.m. 4th Column advanced on their previous line and were halted, as before, by fire from the granary. As this attack faltered, 5th Column renewed theirs but failed to retake the Long Garden. At about 11.00 p.m. fighting around Essling died down and Rosenberg withdrew his columns a short distance from the village to rest.

Fighting had continued through the evening in Aspern as both sides attempted to eject their enemy, but after 9.00 p.m. only sporadic outbreaks flared up, and these had ceased by midnight. Perhaps some 8,000 Austrian soldiers and a much smaller number of French took what shelter they could amid the rubble in the village, grabbing a few hours of respite from the heat of battle and the broiling sun. The exhausted men of both sides rested fitfully amid the flickering flames and bodies of their fallen comrades, the pleading cries of the wounded penetrating the darkness.

▲ *As the Austrian 5th Column prepared to attack Essling at about 8.00 p.m., the cavalry on the left flank, under GM Stutterheim, was ordered to push back the French horsemen of GB Bruyère's brigade. After repeated assaults and numerous mêlées the French cavalry were forced to withdraw, which enabled the Austrian infantry attacks to commence. (K. Foresman).*

▶ *Although this illustration depicts a German infantry regiment incorrectly, wearing the shako, it gives a good impression of the confused and disordered fighting that went on in the village of Aspern. The fighting continued to flare up throughout the evening, finally ceasing at about midnight. (HGM, Vienna).*

Aspern-Essling, 21-22 May 1809; Day Two

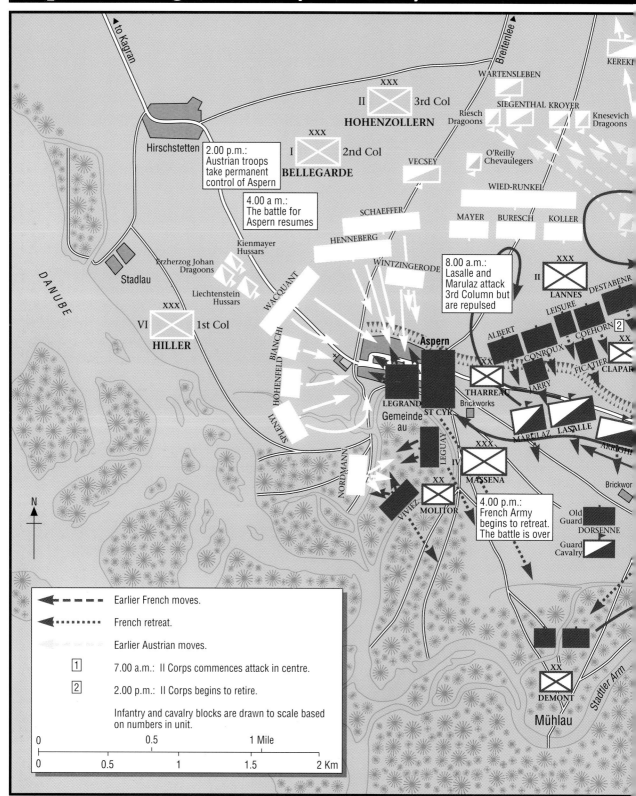

to Kagran

Breitenlee

KEREKI

WARTENSLEBEN

XXX

II 3rd Col

HOHENZOLLERN

SIEGENTHAL KROYER

Riesch
Dragoons

Knesevich
Dragoons

Hirschstetten

2.00 p.m.:
Austrian troops
take permanent
control of Aspern

XXX

I 2nd Col

BELLEGARDE

VECSEY

O'Reilly
Chevaulegers

4.00 a.m.:
The battle for
Aspern resumes

WIED-RUNKEL

SCHAEFFER

MAYER BURESCH KOLLER

Kienmayer
Hussars

HENNEBERG

WINTZINGERODE

8.00 a.m.:
Lasalle and
Marulaz attack
3rd Column but
are repulsed

XXX

II LANNES DESTABENR

Erzherzog Johan
Dragoons

WACQUANT

LEISURE

Stadlau

Liechtenstein
Hussars

ALBERT CONROUX COEHORN [2]

XX

XXX

VI 1st Col

HILLER

HOHENFELD

BIANCHI

Aspern

FICATIER

CLAPAR

JARRY

XX

THARREAU

SPLENYI

Brickworks

MARULAZ LASALLE

LEGRAND ST CYR

ARRIGHI

Gemeinde
au

LEGUAY

NORDMANN

XXX

IV

MASSENA

4.00 p.m.:
French Army
begins to retreat.
The battle is over

Old
Guard

DORSENNE

VIVIEZ

XX

MOLITOR

Guard
Cavalry

Brickwor

N

Earlier French moves.

French retreat.

Earlier Austrian moves.

[1] 7.00 a.m.: II Corps commences attack in centre.

[2] 2.00 p.m.: II Corps begins to retire.

Infantry and cavalry blocks are drawn to scale based
on numbers in unit.

DANUBE

XX

DEMONT

Stadtler Arm

Mühlau

0		0.5		1 Mile	
0	0.5	1	1.5	2 Km	

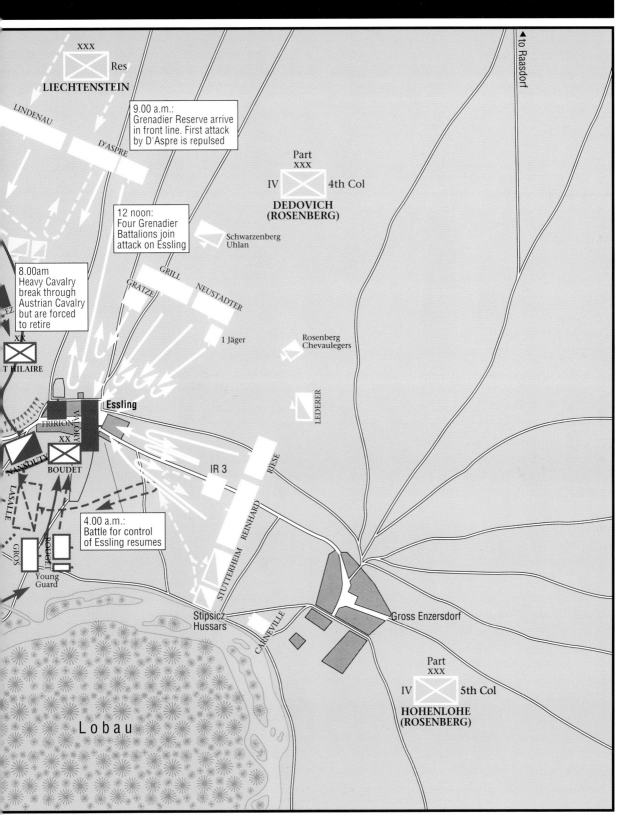

XXX

Res

LIECHTENSTEIN

LINDENAU

D'ASPRE

9.00 a.m.:
Grenadier Reserve arrive
in front line. First attack
by D'Aspre is repulsed

Part
XXX

IV   4th Col

**DEDOVICH
(ROSENBERG)**

12 noon:
Four Grenadier
Battalions join
attack on Essling

Schwarzenberg
Uhlan

GRILL

GRATZE

NEUSTADTER

8.00am
Heavy Cavalry
break through
Austrian Cavalry
but are forced
to retire

1 Jäger

Rosenberg
Chevaulegers

EZ

XX

T HILAIRE

LEDERER

VALORY

Essling

FRIRION

XX

BOUDET

NANSOUTY

IR 3

RIESE

LASALLE

4.00 a.m.:
Battle for control
of Essling resumes

REINHARD

STUTTERHEIM

GROS

ROUGET

Young
Guard

Stipsicz
Hussars

CARNEVILLE

Gross Enzersdorf

Part
XXX

IV   5th Col

**HOHENLOHE
(ROSENBERG)**

L o b a u

▲ to Raasdorf

◄ *Early on the morning of 22 May the French briefly regained control of Aspern but were ejected again by about 5.00 a.m. Massena ordered his men to recapture the village, an attack by Badeners, Hessians and the 24e Légère proving successful. The illustration shows Charles ordering IR14 (Klebek) to retake the shattered buildings from them. After an hour's fighting, the Austrians were forced to withdraw. (F. Wöber).*

The Night of 21/22 May

From about 10.00 p.m. the bridge had become available again, and through the night the eight Young Guard and four Old Guard battalions as well as the divisions of St. Hilaire, Tharreau and Claparède from II Corps passed over the tenuous link. But before Demont's men could join them the connection was again severed. Demont was unable to cross until the early hours of the morning. Meanwhile, Napoleon ordered Davout to assemble III Corps at Kaiser Ebersdorf during the night to be ready to cross the river at the first opportunity.

Charles at his new headquarters in Breitenlee was delighted with the day's effort – unaware of the level of success achieved against the bridge, he believed he had held the whole of Napoleon's army in check. During the night Hohenzollern moved 3rd Column forward a few hundred paces, and the Grenadier Reserve advanced to Breitenlee. The French, with Boudet in Essling and Legrand holding a corner of Aspern, with St. Cyr and Molitor in support, now had the centre covered by Tharreau, Claparède and St. Hilaire. Behind them stood the cavalry; in the rear were the Guard. With his forces increased to about 60,000 infantry, 11,000 cavalry and 152 guns, Napoleon now planned to go on the offensive and break the Austrian centre with Lannes' II Corps.

22 May 1809: Second Day.

While the early morning mist still clung to the battlefield prior to sunrise, Napoleon was awake and issuing orders to set his new plan in motion. For the attack against the centre to succeed he needed to hold on to Essling and recapture Aspern to secure his flanks.

By 4.00 a.m. the fighting was as fierce as ever. Six French battalions smashed into the main part of Aspern, throwing back the startled Austrians, but as the impetus of the attack slowed a counter-attack surged forward and bundled the French back to their starting line by 5.00 a.m. Massena, determined to regain control, ordered the 24ème Légère and the Baden IR3 (Graf Hochberg) to attack, supported by Schinner's Hessian brigade. A vicious struggle for supremacy ensued, the two sides surging back and forth through the ruins until, at about 7.00 a.m., Massena's men were masters of the whole village once more.

Essling also erupted into furious action early in the morning, an artillery bombardment and an attack by Lasalle's cavalry forcing the Austrians farther back toward Gross-Enzersdorf. Rosenberg ordered a counter-offensive by his two columns, IR3 (Erzherzog Karl), transferred from 4th Column, spearheading one attack by Reinhard's brigade of 5th Column. The advance was met by heavy musketry and artillery fire from Boudet's men, followed by a cavalry attack. The Austrians, forming battalion masses, stood firm until supporting hussars drove the French troopers off. Dedovich led 4th Column forward but halted in masses outside the village, opening up with his artillery. However, this gave time for the French artillerymen to train their pieces on these tightly packed formations and to carve great lanes of destruction through the vulnerable infantry. To avoid this unproductive slaughter, Dedovich ordered his men into Essling, but the arrival of part of the Young Guard was enough to dislodge his weak grip on the village. By 7.00 a.m., with both flanks secure, Napoleon was ready to smash decisively through the centre of the Austrian position.

The French Breakthrough Attempt

At Aspern that morning Charles first learnt of the effectiveness of the attempts to destroy the bridges, and as the morning mist lifted he became aware that the main French assault was to be aimed at his centre. Ordering Hiller and Bellegarde to recapture Aspern at any cost, he rode off to meet this new threat personally.

By 7.00 a.m. Lannes' three assault divisions were in position along the Aspern–Essling road. The divisions were to advance *en echelon* with St. Hilaire's on the right leading, accompanied by Lannes, while Oudinot would bring forward Claparède and Tharreau. By smashing the centre and forcing it back on its right, Napoleon intended to push Davout's III Corps through the resulting gap to achieve another crushing victory.

Spearheaded by the fearsome 57ème Ligne, and with artillery support, St. Hilaire's division began to advance. Behind the infantry formed the light cavalry of Marulaz and Lasalle and the heavy cavalry of Nansouty and Arrighi, who had replaced the mortally wounded d'Espagne.

As the advance rolled slowly forward, some Austrian battalions in the front line began to waver and pull back; rallied in the rear, they were ordered to return and extend the left of the line. Meanwhile the numerically superior Austrian artillery had begun to pour a devastating fire into the oncoming French, checking their forward movement. To break this deadlock the French cavalry were ordered forward. The light cavalry repeatedly assaulted the masses of 3rd Column on the left but were unable to break their resistance and eventually retreated, leaving many prisoners to the Austrians. On the right the heavy cavalry attack appeared more successful, targeted as on the previous day against the junction between Hohenzollern's men and the Reserve Cavalry. The onslaught caused the Austrian cavalry to fall back and seek protection among the infantry masses. In the third line, two regiments of Insurrec-

▶ *To relieve pressure on the French infantry assault, pinned down by artillery fire, French cavalry launched attacks against the Austrian line. At this critical moment, exposed to artillery and cavalry attacks, elements of IR15 (Zach) were wavering when Charles rode up, steadied the men and encouraged the line to stand and repulse the attacks. (Hulton-Deutsch Collection).*

Major of the French 100ème de Ligne. The 4th battalion of this unit formed a part of the 2nd Division of II Corps and was heavily involved at Aspern and in the attempt to capture Baumersdorf during the Battle of Wagram.(Bryan Fosten)

tio cavalry, the Primatial and Neutraer Hussars, panicked and fled.

The critical point in the battle had been reached. In the midst of the heavy cavalry attack stood the first battalion of IR15 (Zach), one of the units that had already withdrawn, rallied and been sent to the left. They had stood their ground against the cuirassiers, but as the cavalry moved on they found themselves confronted at close range by French artillery that had moved up, screened by the horsemen. As the guns opened up, the battalion collapsed and made for the rear, only a body of 200 men grouped around an officer awaiting their fate. With a hole about to open in the centre, Charles appeared, supervising the advance of the Grenadier Reserve. Spurring into the broken elements of IR15, he is reputed to have seized their standard, rallied them and led them back into battle, thus securing the line. Whatever truth there is in this incident, it has certainly passed into Austrian military lore. Whether Charles actually did take the standard will never be known for sure – he modestly denied it later. What is certain is that Charles' intervention stabilized the line, and the critical moment passed. With the Austrian line firm again, the French cuirassiers, fired on at close range and attacked by Austrian cavalry, fled back behind their own stationary infantry.

By 9.00 a.m., Lannes' men, suffering mounting casualties and low on ammunition, could not be induced to advance again. Lannes' request for reinforcements reached Napoleon at the same time as news of another rupture of the bridge – this time it had carried away a party of engineers. It was now impossible for Davout's III Corps to cross; there would be no reinforcements.

The arrival of the Grenadier Reserve in the centre threatened to make matters worse for Lannes, as FML d'Aspre's division advanced against St. Hilaire's right, but a timely movement by Fririon's brigade from Essling, firing a close-range volley into the grenadiers' flank, forced them back in disorder. Charles, again close to the danger, restored order in their ranks. Nagging cavalry attacks and heavy firing began to induce a grudging rearward movement by the French line, news of a fresh breaking of the bridge adding to a lowering of morale. There were reports of men feigning injury, leaving the line and making their own way back to the river. Among the casualties was St. Hilaire, mortally wounded when his left foot was shot away. By midday the French were back behind the Aspern–Essling road; the great breakthrough attempt had failed. The grenadier divisions of d'Aspre and FML Lindenau relieved Hohenzollern's men in the front line as the French looked nervously to the security of their flanks.

Renewed Assaults on Aspern and Essling

The French assault on the centre had got under way at 7.00 a.m. At the same time the renewal of the Austrian attack on Aspern was heralded by a barrage from the artillery of 1st and 2nd Columns. Led by a battalion of IR51 (Splényi), a major new assault stormed back into the village, the defenders thrown back by the violence of the attack. With ammunition running low, the combatants armed themselves with anything that came to hand. Massena, seeing that the Austrians were gaining the advantage, fed in his last reserve, a battalion of Hessian Leib-Garde, which halted their progress. At about 8.00 a.m., Austrian howitzers began dropping shells into the French-held portion of the village, rekindling the flames that had died down and forcing the occupants to evacuate. Following the lifting of the barrage, the Hessians rushed back into the village and almost cleared it of defenders, but

▲ *Repeated Austrian assaults failed to capture the massive stone-built granary at Essling. Here Grenadiers of the Georgy battalion from IR42 and IR36 are about to be* *repulsed by Boudet's men amidst heavy casualties. (Romain Baulesch)*

▶ *Having led the Grenadier Reserve forward, Charles ordered Hohenzollern's 3rd Column to withdraw, allowing him to position the grenadiers in the front line. The arrival of these fresh troops in the centre increased the preasure on Lannes' shaken troops. (HGM, Vienna).*

◄ *Forced to evacuate Aspern by howitzer fire, the French and their German allies regrouped. At 10.00 a.m. an attack spearheaded by 2nd Batt. Hessian Leib Regiment recaptured the village once more. The illustration shows the next counter-attack by IR31 (Benjowsky) and IR51 (Splényi), which regained control again briefly before they were themselves ejected. (F. Wöber).*

◄ *With the failure of 4th and 5th Columns to capture Essling, Charles ordered four battalions of grenadiers to join the assault. Charging forward into a heavy fire from Boudet's men, they threw themselves at the high walls of the Great Garden and the stone granary, suffering fearful casulties. (HGM, Vienna).*

◄ *At about 3.00 p.m. GdK Liechtenstein planned a coordinated attack against Essling, which suceeded in gaining control of the village. Although the granary remained in Boudet's hands, the majority of his exhausted division were driven out.*

◀ *Around midday with the French in control of Aspern, volunteers were called for a renewed attack. Three hundred men from IR31 (Ben-jowsky) and IR14 (Kle-bek) stepped forward and assaulted the cemetery. The illustration shows Korporal Bollogh of IR31 about to claim the honour of being the first over the wall. Heavily supported, this attack succeeded. (F. Wöber)*

IR51 (Spényi) and a battalion of IR31 (Benjowsky) fought back and recaptured the church and cemetery. At 11.00 a.m. the Austrians were back in complete control, only to lose it again as three battalions of Young Guard tirailleurs from Essling joined the fray. But by 1.00 p.m. the Austrians had regained mastery of the village. The French threw in a last major assault just after 1.00 p.m., the desperate fighting at its most bitter as the battle-crazed soldiers tore at each other, in some cases with their bare hands. With the French reserves committed and their men exhausted after almost 24 hours of continual fighting, the Austrians finally became masters of the smoking mounds of rubble that had been Aspern.

With the threat to the centre removed, Charles ordered a renewed assault on Essling. This time Rosenberg's columns were to be reinforced by three grenadier battalions from d'Aspre's division and one from Lindenau's. The grenadiers advanced through Boudet's fire right up to the high walls of the Great Garden, where they thrust bayonets through the loopholes to get to grips with the defenders and attempted to hack their way through the heavy iron door of the granary. But the attacks by 4th and 5th Columns were again uncoordinated, and all the assaults were beaten off. While the men were re-forming, Liechtenstein arrived and instilled new courage in them before organizing the first properly coordinated attack on the village, Charles appearing in time to lead the grenadiers forward. The triple thrust burst into Essling, overwhelming Boudet's overstretched and exhausted division at 3.00 p.m. – although the granary, with Boudet inside, held out.

Between 1.00 and 2.00 p.m., preparations for an Austrian counter-offensive in the centre were made. Almost 200 guns placed in the front line opened a

▶ *Between 1.00 p.m. and 2.00 p.m. the Austrians formed a massive artillery battery of almost two hundred guns across their centre, facing the French infantry. The weight of fire directed at these men soon began to tell, their line being forced back by heavy casulties. (K. Foresman).*

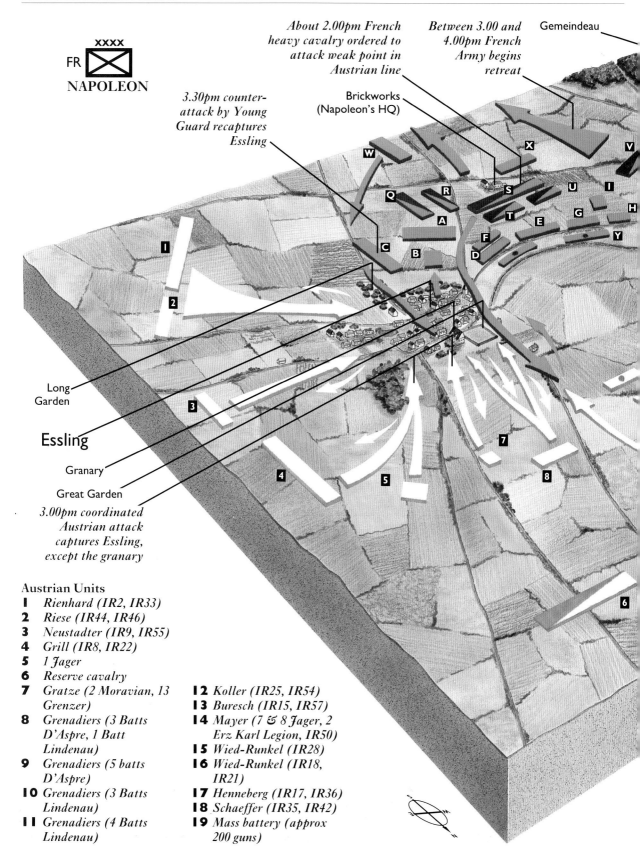

FR ⊠ xxxx

NAPOLEON

About 2.00pm French heavy cavalry ordered to attack weak point in Austrian line

Between 3.00 and 4.00pm French Army begins retreat

Gemeindeau

3.30pm counter-attack by Young Guard recaptures Essling

Brickworks (Napoleon's HQ)

Long Garden

Essling

Granary

Great Garden

3.00pm coordinated Austrian attack captures Essling, except the granary

Austrian Units

1 Rienhard (IR2, IR33)
2 Riese (IR44, IR46)
3 Neustadter (IR9, IR55)
4 Grill (IR8, IR22)
5 1 Jager
6 Reserve cavalry
7 Gratze (2 Moravian, 13 Grenzer)
8 Grenadiers (3 Batts D'Aspre, 1 Batt Lindenau)
9 Grenadiers (5 batts D'Aspre)
10 Grenadiers (3 Batts Lindenau)
11 Grenadiers (4 Batts Lindenau)

12 Koller (IR25, IR54)
13 Buresch (IR15, IR57)
14 Mayer (7 & 8 Jager, 2 Erz Karl Legion, IR50)
15 Wied-Runkel (IR28)
16 Wied-Runkel (IR18, IR21)
17 Henneberg (IR17, IR36)
18 Schaeffer (IR35, IR42)
19 Mass battery (approx 200 guns)

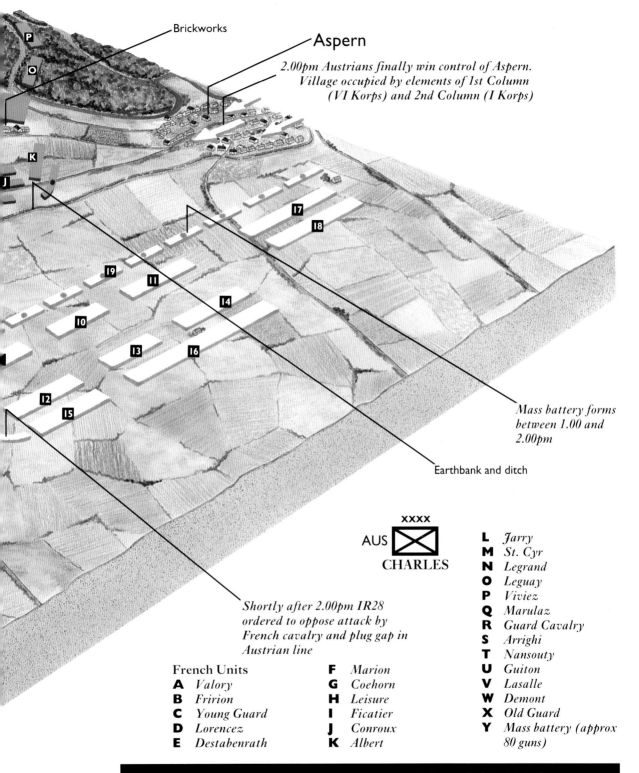

Brickworks

Aspern

2.00pm Austrians finally win control of Aspern.
Village occupied by elements of 1st Column
(VI Korps) and 2nd Column (I Korps)

Mass battery forms
between 1.00 and
2.00pm

Earthbank and ditch

xxxx

AUS [⊠]

CHARLES

Shortly after 2.00pm IR28
ordered to oppose attack by
French cavalry and plug gap in
Austrian line

French Units

A	*Valory*	**F**	*Marion*
B	*Fririon*	**G**	*Coehorn*
C	*Young Guard*	**H**	*Leisure*
D	*Lorencez*	**I**	*Ficatier*
E	*Destabenrath*	**J**	*Conroux*
		K	*Albert*

L	*Jarry*
M	*St. Cyr*
N	*Legrand*
O	*Leguay*
P	*Viviez*
Q	*Marulaz*
R	*Guard Cavalry*
S	*Arrighi*
T	*Nansouty*
U	*Guiton*
V	*Lasalle*
W	*Demont*
X	*Old Guard*
Y	*Mass battery (approx 80 guns)*

THE BATTLE OF ASPERN–ESSLING

Napoleon's last attempt to prevent defeat, 2.00–4.00pm 22 May 1809

◀ To counter a threatened Austrian attack in the centre, Napoleon ordered a combined attack against a gap in their line. Spearheaded by the cuirassiers, the charge was met by the Austrians drawn up in battalion masses, which stood firm against the attack. Although the French were repulsed, this aggresive tactic shook the Austrians, who showed a reluctance to advance further.

◀ The Austrian occupation of Essling had been short-lived. Half an hour later General Mouton led a counter-attack of the Young Guard which, after desperate fighting and heavy losses on both sides, cleared the village of Austrians and relieved the granary. (P. J. Haythornthwaite).

◀ The Austrian grenadiers, now ejected from Essling, re-formed and made one more attack against the village. Following the failure of this assault, Charles issued orders forbidding any further attack by the grenadiers. The shattered units withdrew, the Scovaud battalion numbering only 160 fit men while Kirchenbetter's could only muster 46. (P. J. Haythornthwaite).

relentless fire upon the French troops, forcing Oudinot's men to pull back with heavy losses. Even Napoleon was in danger of being hit. The French artillery, about 80 guns, attempted to protect the infantry while the Old Guard awaited developments in reserve, behind the cavalry. All along the line the French edged back. In a final effort to hold off the Austrians, Napoleon launched a combined attack against a gap that had appeared in the Austrian line. Ordered into the threatened position, IR28 (Frelich) hurried forward in battalion masses and fought off the attack, but this aggressive act by the French induced a reluctance in the Austrian line to advance again. At 2.30 p.m. the bridge became operational once more, resulting in scenes of disorder as French wounded and deserters struggled to cross to safety against the already restricted flow of traffic. It proved necessary to deploy a battalion of Old Guard at the bridge to restore order – but the bridge gave way soon after.

The Austrian occupation of Essling at 3.00 p.m. was short-lived. Within half an hour, Général Mouton led a counter-attack by one battalion of tirailleurs and two battalions of fusilier chasseurs of the Young Guard, supported by two battalions of fusilier grenadiers, and retook the entire village. The Austrian grenadiers in turn reformed and launched their fifth separate attack against Essling. Devastated by the continual exposure to enemy fire and at one stage that of their own artillery, they were forbidden by Charles to storm the village again. It was reported that the Kirchenbetter battalion, which had started the battle about 600 strong, was reduced to 46 fit men.

The French Retreat

Charles, now concerned about his own mounting casualties and shortage of ammunition, ordered the centre to withdraw a short distance and reorganize. At Aspern, the French continued to harass the Austrian defenders: unable to gain the village themselves, they at least managed to prevent Hiller's men emerging from it. At about 4.00 p.m., Napoleon withdrew to the Danube and organized the final retreat, during which his great friend, Lannes, had both his legs smashed by a cannonball; this was to cause his death a week later.

The battered French fell back to the Lobau, only intermittent skirmishing opposing their move as Charles had ordered that further conflict should be avoided. Peace was now uppermost in his mind. The death and destruction had been immense. On a narrow battle front less than four kilometres wide, almost 45,000 casualties had spilt their blood for the eagles of Austria and France. The Habsburg army reported 4,286 dead, 16,314 wounded, 837 captured and 1,903 missing. French estimates are rather vague but it is likely that about 7,000 were killed and maybe more than 16,000 wounded. Napoleon's rashness and underestimation of Austria's resolve had enabled Charles to inflict on him his first defeat. Word spread like wildfire across Europe. But while Charles now hoped to bring about a peaceful

▶ *During the French retreat Napoleon's great friend Lannes was hit by a cannonball, which smashed his knees, necessitating the amputation of his right leg. Lannes' premonition that he would be hit that day had been fulfilled. His condition worsened as the wound became infected, and nine days later he died. (F. Wöber).*

settlement, Napoleon set to with a single-minded determination to avenge his defeat.

The Aftermath of Battle

Napoleon crossed the Danube by boat at about 1.00 a.m. on 23 May, leaving the army to seek what shelter it could on Lobau, a great thunderstorm making their misery complete. Soaked to the skin, the exhausted soldiers lay amongst the dead and dying, with little to eat except horse flesh and nettles, flavoured with gunpowder and boiled in upturned cavalry cuirasses.

Without a decisive victory, personal rivalry and jealousy reappeared within the Austrian political and military hierarchy, as support for peace or a continuation of the war was argued and debated. A number of plans for an Austrian river crossing were discussed but came to nothing, while Charles pulled the army away from the increasingly unhealthy battlefield to a position behind the Russbach stream to await developments. Hiller's VI Korps and Klenau's Advance Guard remained to observe movements on

the Danube and began construction of a series of defensive redoubts mainly in the Aspern to Gross-Enzersdorf area.

Charles now received 7,000 Landwehr recruits, and from his new headquarters at Deutsch-Wagram he organized their training before brigading them with regular units. He also recalled two divisions of III Korps that had been left to cover the retreat through Bohemia. Charles was unable to recall Archduke Ferdinand from the north, as a move by Russian troops into Habsburg territory in Galicia had necessitated a withdrawal from Poland to oppose any further incursions. The only other possible reinforcement would therefore be the force of Archduke John. His advance into Italy had halted with the collapse of the campaign in Bavaria and his orders to retire and cover the flank of Charles' army. Pressure from Eugène's Army of Italy and Marmont's Army of Dalmatia had forced John back to Graz, where he hoped to link with the division returning from the occupation of Munich. But this force was defeated *en route*, with only a few survivors making the rendezvous. Retiring into Hungary, John was joined by a large Insurrectio force but was defeated at Raab on 14 June before retreating to the Danube crossing at Pressburg (Bratislava). John's leisurely manoeuvring had angered Charles, who had urged his brother to use all speed to link up with the main army. Archduke John would not arrive on the Marchfeld for the next great battle – but his pursuers, Eugène and Marmont, would.

Having eventually evacuated all but IV Corps from Lobau, Napoleon ordered a large number of guns, many from the arsenal in Vienna, to be placed on the island to strengthen it, and commenced the construction of two great bridges across the Danube. Boosted by the arrival of Eugène and Marmont, Napoleon ordered forward Wrede's Bavarian division from VII Corps, Bernadotte's IX (Saxon) Corps, and was delighted by the arrival of the Guard Artillery after its long march. By early July,

▶ *In the early hours of 23 May, with the bridge once more out of operation, Napoleon was rowed across the Danube to Kaiser Ebersdorf. Included in his party were Berthier and a fatally wounded Austrian officer, FML Wöber. The French army withdrew to Lobau and spent a miserable night, cold and hungry in the heavy rain. (F. Wöber).*

▶ *Centre: The Austrian staff at the Battle of Aspern– Essling. The village of Aspern can be seen burning in the right background. The central group, left to right, are: Archduke Charles, Liechtenstein, Wimpffen (chief of Staff), Hiller, Bellegarde, Hohenzollern and Rosenberg. (HGM, Vienna).*

▶ *Below: Archduke John, aged 27 in 1809, was a younger brother of Charles. When only 18 he had commanded the army in Bavaria but was defeated at Hohenlinden. At the outbreak of war in 1809 he was given command of VIII and IX Korps in northern Italy, but his dilatory manoeuvring angered Charles. (D. Hollins).*

six weeks after his defeat at Aspern–Essling, Napoleon had gathered a massive army of 190,500 men and 617 guns. Across the river with 137,700 men and 414 guns, Charles awaited Napoleon's next move. Still hoping for a peaceful settlement, he pondered the failure of the pre-conditions of victory: Prussia had not joined the war; there had been no popular rising in Germany; Russia was now appearing aggressive in Galicia; and the promised British diversionary attack had failed to materialize. Standing alone, and with the failure of the peace initiatives, Charles resigned himself to 'strike one more blow against the French'.

THE BATTLE OF WAGRAM

Return to the Marchfeld

To ensure there would be no repeat of the disastrous river crossing in May, Napoleon's bridging of the Danube this time was meticulously planned and executed. The first stretch of river to Schneidergrund was spanned by two well-constructed bridges, these also crossing the second stretch to Lobgrund with an additional smaller bridge for infantry only. To prevent any Austrian attempts at disrupting the traffic, a line of poles was driven into the river bed to shield the new constructions and twenty boats were assigned to patrolling the river.

Napoleon hoped to convince the Austrians that he intended crossing in the same area as before. To this end he erected a pontoon bridge and sent Legrand's division over to construct some earthworks on the Mühlau, while he completed arrangements for a crossing from the eastern side of Lobau.

Charles reacted to this deception by advancing across the ripening cornfields of the Marchfeld on 1 July and forming his army behind the advance troops and redoubts, closer to the Mühlau. With his line now coming under heavy artillery fire from Lobau, Charles realised the danger in fighting too close to the river; unsure of Napoleon's intentions, he ordered the withdrawal of the army back to their positions beyond the Russbach and below the Bisamberg on 2 July, leaving Hiller's VI Korps and Klenau's Advance Guard alone and isolated again on the Danube. Hiller, who had often quarrelled with Charles, was extremely unhappy about the situation. He had complained on a number of occasions about his lack of strength with which to oppose a major French move, and the weakness of his position; finally on 4 July he informed Charles that he could no longer command VI Korps due to ill health. Hiller was replaced on the eve of battle by FML Klenau of the Advance Guard, Klenau's own position being taken by Nordmann, who had led

◀ *The bridging oper- ation for the second crossing of the Danube was meticulously planned in order to avoid the errors of May. As well as a floating bridge, the first stretch of the river was to be spanned by a strong pile bridge. The illustr- ation shows Napoleon supervising the construct- ion of this bridge; the village of Kaiser Ebersdorf is visible in the background. (P. J. Haythornthwaite).*

▶ *The second stretch of the Danube, between Schneidergrund and Lobgrund, was spanned by three bridges. The illustration shows the two pile bridges in operation. The main bridge, on the right, was 3.7 metres wide and intended for all traffic; the bridge on the left was for infantry only, being just 1.6 metres wide. (Anne S. K. Brown Collection).*

Hiller's own advance guard at Aspern, now promoted to FML.

Charles finally accepted that the forthcoming French main attack would be launched from the Lobau when he received news that a large body of troops (one of Davout's divisions, which had been occupying Archduke John's attention) was

▼ *FML Johann Count Klenau had commanded II Korps Advance Guard in the opening stages of the campaign and the Advance Guard of 4th Column at Aspern–Essling. As the forces gathered prior to Wagram, he commanded the Army Advance Guard, but following Hiller's resignation was appointed commander of VI Korps on the eve of battle. (HGM, Vienna)*

advancing towards the bridge at Kaiser Ebersdorf from the direction of Pressburg, and that another large group, Bernadotte's Saxons, were already crossing on to the island. At 2.00 p.m. on 5 July the skies darkened and a crash of thunder heralded a tremendous downpour, which dowsed all the camp fires and ensured a wet miserable afternoon for all.

The position occupied by the Habsburg army was a reasonably strong one. The Marchfeld was a vast flat plain, its occasional areas of higher ground, rising only a metre or two, being hardly detectable from a distance. At the northern extreme of the plain ran the narrow Russbach stream, its steep, tree-lined banks presenting an obstacle to both cavalry and artillery. Beyond the stream an area of boggy ground, about 100 metres wide, led to the major feature of the Marchfeld, an escarpment varying between 10 and 20 metres in height, known as the Wagram, which lay between the villages of Deutsch-Wagram and Markgrafneusiedl. To the west of the village of Wagram the ground began to rise gently behind Gerasdorf and Stammersdorf to the heights of the Bisamberg, which overlooked the Danube.

Charles, having dropped the Column designations and returned to corps titles, had deployed I, II and IV Korps on the escarpment behind the Russbach. From Wagram there was an open space of about five kilometres before the Grenadier Reserve position in front of Seyring. III Korps were at Hagenbrunn, while V Korps occupied the Bisamberg, Schwarzen Lackenau and the banks of the Danube towards Krems. About eight kilometres ahead of these positions stood VI

◄ *A modern photograph of the Russbach stream, which has changed little in appearance since 1809. Although narrow, the steep, tree-lined banks presented a difficult obstacle for cavalry and an impossible one for the French artillery.*

the Russbach, those corps positioned there would hold them while the corps from the Bisamberg area would advance into the enemy's left flank. If Napoleon directed his assault towards the Bisamberg, the corps there would hold him while those on the Russbach would swing into his right.

At 7.00 p.m. on 4 July, aware that the French had weakened their position at Pressburg, Charles sent a message to Archduke John ordering him to leave enough troops to defend the river and move with all speed, initially to Marchegg on the March river. 'The battle here on the Marchfeld will determine the fate of our Dynasty.... I request you march here at once, leaving behind all baggage and impedimenta, and join my left wing.' The onset of heavy thunderstorms delayed delivery of the message until 6.00 a.m. the following morning.

At 9.00 p.m., under cover of freezing rain, the French began to cross, slowly at first as small boats ferried men to the far bank, but soon great bridges appeared across the Stadtler Arm. While a thunderstorm raged overhead and the cannon on Lobau echoed its anger, Oudinot, Massena and Davout led their corps through the dripping trees that lined the river on to the Marchfeld, the dark night lit only by the glow of the burning village of

Korps and the Advance Guard, supported by the Reserve Cavalry. These two advanced corps were ordered to oppose any French movement on the Marchfeld with the utmost vigour, delaying them as much as possible before falling back, VI Korps on the Bisamberg and the Advance Guard on Markgrafneusiedl.

Charles' battle plan was simple. If the French entered the Marchfeld and headed for the line of

◄ *This photograph taken from the banks of the Russbach shows the boggy area, about 100 metres wide, which the French troops crossed before assaulting the Austrian positions on the escarpment. The photograph was taken between the villages of Deutsch-Wagram and Baumersdorf (Parbesdorf).*

► *Voltigeur cornet of the 18ème de Ligne and Voltgeur of 3ème de Ligne. Three battalions of the 18ème took part in the ferocious street fighting in Aspern, forming part of Massena's IV Corps. At Wagram they took part in the fierce battle for control of Aderklaa. The 3ème formed part of the 3rd Division of II Corps at both battles. (Bryan Fosten)*

Gross-Enzersdorf, set alight by French shells. The Battle of Wagram had begun.

5 July 1809: The First Day

Oudinot, now in command of II Corps again following the death of Lannes, led his men forward, encountering elements of the 1tes Jäger and pushing these outnumbered light troops back until they reached Sachsengang Castle where, with 7tes Jäger, they barricaded themselves in and held out until their ammunition was exhausted. FML Nordmann, alerted by the French bombardment, formed the Advance Guard to obstruct the French movement. Three battalions occupied Gross-Enzersdorf and the adjacent earthworks, while the brigades of Riese and Mayer formed up behind the village.

To ease the congestion as the French began to form their attack lines it became necessary for them to capture this village, providing as it did the pivot on which Napoleon would swing his great army on to the central Marchfeld. In accordance with this, Massena pushed his men forward against the burning buildings. Nordmann opposed this move with IR58 (Beaulieu), who after making some headway were forced back to the village at about 5.00 a.m. An attack spearheaded by 46ème Ligne ultimately met with success after fierce hand-to-hand fighting among the ruins and earthworks. With the village firmly in French hands, Nordmann fell back to Essling.

Charles at Wagram, receiving news of the French movement at 5.00 a.m., ordered defences to be dug along the Russbach line at Markgrafneusiedl and Baumersdorf (Parbesdorf). At 5.30 a.m. he wrote to John again instructing him to march to Markgrafneusiedl, after three hours' rest at Marchegg. Unfortunately John had still not received Charles' first dispatch – it finally arrived at 6.00 a.m. And even though Charles had urged John to make haste it took a further nineteen hours for him to collect together his dispersed command and prepare to march to the battle.

Klenau and Nordmann now waited for Napoleon's next move, while Liechtenstein's Reserve Cavalry occupied the space between them and the main army. The cavalry divisions of Schwarzenberg and Nostitz were at Pysdorf, GM Roussel's cuiras-

sier brigade was at Neu Wirsthaus, while Lederer and Kroyer's cuirassier brigades were in reserve at Raasdorf.

Unsure as to whether he just faced a rearguard protecting a move north by Charles with the main army, Napoleon probed forward with three light cavalry brigades just after midday. The cavalry first moved towards Rutzendorf, which some of Davout's men then occupied , before swinging towards Pysdorf, where they encountered the Austrian cavalry, though neither side appears to have sought confrontation.

Advance Across the Marchfeld

Napoleon was now ready to launch his army forward, on the left the light cavalry of Lasalle and Marulaz, to their right IV Corps (Massena), II Corps (Oudinot) and finally III Corps (Davout), with the far right protected by the dragoon divisions of Grouchy and Pully. By 2.00 p.m. the hot sun had long since burnt off the early morning mist, leaving nothing to mask Klenau and Nordmann's dramatic view of this great army as it began to move through the gently waving fields of corn. Concerned by the presence of French cavalry to his left rear, Nordmann started a stubborn withdrawal towards Markgrafneusiedl, protected by Liechtenstein's cavalry. As IV Corps' initial move was a great wheel to the left, pivoting on Boudet's division, Klenau was able to hold his position for some time before conducting a spirited and orderly withdrawal to Stammersdorf. With this manoeuvre complete, Massena pushed forward with his corps to a position north-west of Aspern at Breitenlee with detachments further ahead at Kagran, Leopoldau and Süssenbrunn. Oudinot was to march to a position on the Russbach opposite Baumersdorf, and Davout was to move towards Markgrafneusiedl via Glinzendorf. As the three French corps fanned out across the Marchfeld, a large gap opened between Massena and Oudinot into which Eugène with the Army of Italy and Bernadotte with the Saxons of IX Corps were pushed. A forward element of IX Corps, GD Dupas' mixed French and Saxon division, clashed with Riese's brigade of Nordmann's Advance Guard and the Wallachisch-Illyrisches Grenzer about 3.30 p.m. at Raasdorf, easily ejecting

▶ *A modern photograph taken from the outskirts of Baumersdorf (Parbesdorf), which clearly illustrates the totally featureless nature of the Marchfeld, across which Oudinot's men had to advance to attack the village.*

the Austrian defenders. Passing Raasdorf, the main body of the corps pushed on towards Aderklaa until at about 5.00 p.m. their left was threatened by Roussel's cuirassier brigade. The two regiments, about 1,000 strong, deployed in two lines, the Herzog Albert on the left and Erzherzog Franz on the right. To counter this danger the Saxon cavalry began to form for a charge but, perhaps seeking personal glory, four squadrons of the Prinz Clemens Chevauxlegers, about 400 men, rushed forward alone. Contrary to the practice of the day, the Austrian cavalry stood to receive the charge, the second rank discharging their pistols at 30 metres, totally destroying the impetus of the charge and repulsing the Saxons. The main force of Saxon cavalry now came forward *en echelon* with the right leading. The Austrians, although now outnumbered, chose to receive the charge with firepower again. This time they failed, and the ordered ranks of horsemen dissolved into a great mêlée of individual combats. Amongst the Saxon cavalry was a single squadron of Herzog Albrecht (Albert) Chevauxlegers, which shared the same Inhaber or Regimental Proprietor as the Austrian Herzog Albert Cuirassier; both were now immersed in the struggle. After a few minutes the Austrian cavalry broke from the mêlée, retreating beyond Aderklaa, their ride to safety secured by the intervention of Lederer's cuirassier brigade.

On the far right, Davout had occupied the village of Glinzendorf, south of Markgrafneusiedl, while Grouchy and Pully's dragoons tentatively probed to the east for signs of Archduke John's approach from Pressburg.

The French Assault on the Wagram

The first stage of Napoleon's plan was now complete. The French army was arrayed in a great sweep from the Danube and Aspern on the left, through Breitenlee, Süssenbrunn and Aderklaa, before swinging to the right along the Russbach stream towards Markgrafneusiedl. Behind the line stood the Imperial Guard in reserve. Opposite them, with the disadvantage of holding the outside line, the Austrian position stretched for nearly 20 kilometres. The largest battle the world had yet seen was about to begin in earnest.

As it was now about 6.00 p.m., Charles and his staff assumed that the battle would begin at first light the next day. But Napoleon was already issuing orders for an immediate attack. With the majority of the Austrian forces north of the Russbach out of sight, drawn back beyond the lip of the escarpment, Napoleon still did not know what strength opposed him or whether the Austrians would stand or retire. In an effort to drive a wedge into the Austrian line, he ordered Bernadotte, Eugène, Oudinot and Davout to attack between the villages of Deutsch-Wagram and Markgrafneusiedl that evening.

The peace of the warm summer's evening was shattered at 7.00 p.m. when the French batteries sent out a thunderous barrage of iron towards the Austrian positions, the village of Baumersdorf in the

61

centre of the Russbach line suffering much from this onslaught. Although all around them the buildings erupted into flames, the defenders, 8tes Jäger and a battalion of Volunteers of the Erzherzog Karl Legion, held firm under GM Hardegg and defended themselves vigorously. Oudinot, who was attacking the village, was unable to force his way in with Frère's (formally Claparède's) division, so he launched a flanking attack to the right of the village at about 8.00 p.m. with 10ème Légère and 57ème Ligne. The 57ème smashed their way into the houses on the eastern side of the village but were unable to make any further progress against the defenders, who stubbornly held on behind every wall and building. Passing the village, the 10ème Légère crossed the stream and boggy area below the escarpment, and struggled up the steep incline. On reaching the top they found themselves confronted by Buresch's brigade of II Korps. Disordered by their advance, the French infantry were now exposed to heavy musketry followed by a charge of the Vincent's Chevauxlegers led by Hohenzollern in person. Alone and unsupported, the 10ème Légère fled back down the escarpment and past Baumersdorf, taking the 57ème with them, and eventually re-forming towards Raasdorf.

A gentle breeze blowing from the east provided excellent cover for the attack of the Army of Italy to the left of Baumersdorf, as the smoke from the burning village drifted across their line of march. Dupas' mixed division, now temporarily attached to the Army of Italy, led the advance up the escarpment before moving to their left toward Wagram. Macdonald followed with Lamarque's division supported by the divisions of Serras and Durette as well as Sahuc's cavalry, which found a way across the stream. The sudden appearance of the French cresting the escarpment caused the Austrian artillery to panic and abandon their guns, fleeing back on the infantry of Bellegarde's I Korps. Lamarque's division pressed on, attacking IR47 (Vogelsang), which broke, taking a battalion of IR11 (Erzherzog Rainer) with them, continuing into a battalion of IR35 (Argenteau) in the second line.

Meanwhile some of Dupas' men were attacking the easternmost buildings of Wagram. The position on the escarpment was looking dangerous for I Korps, but Bellegarde now displayed good

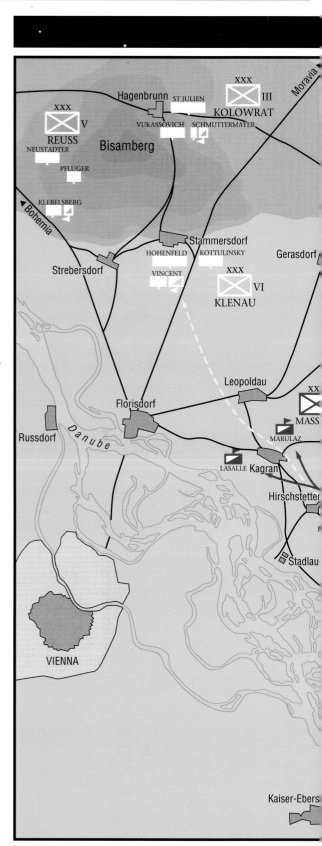

Wagram, 5-6 July 1809: Day One

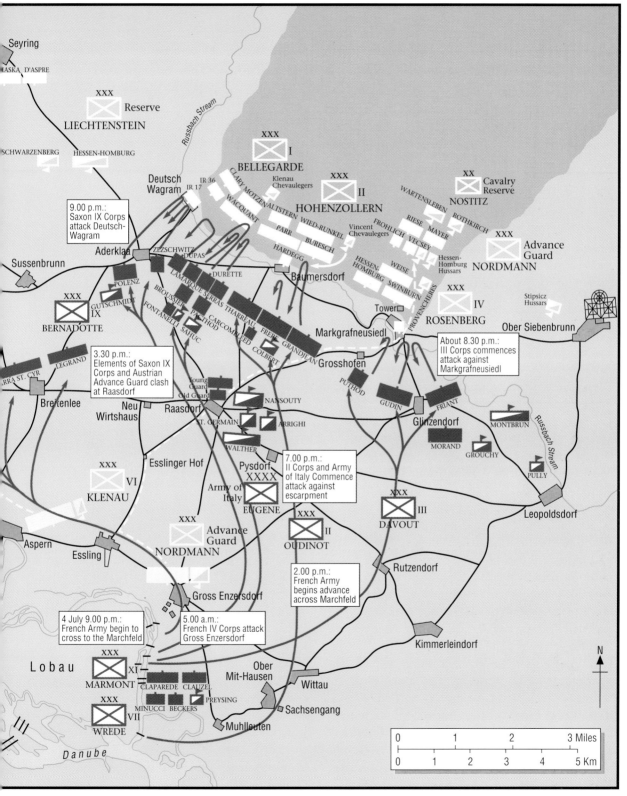

Seyring

LASKA D'ASPRE

XXX Reserve
LIECHTENSTEIN

SCHWARZENBERG   HESSEN-HOMBURG

Deutsch
Wagram   IR 36
            IR 17

XXX I
BELLEGARDE

Klenau
Chevaulegers

CLARY MOTZEN ALISTERN WIED-RUNKEL
WACQUANT
PARR
BURESCH
HARDEGG

XXX II
HOHENZOLLERN

WARTENSLEBEN
ROTHKIRCH
RIESE MAYER
FROHLICH VECSEY
Vincent
Chevaulegers
WEISE
HESSEN-
HOMBURG SWINBURN
Hessen-
Homburg
Hussars

XX Cavalry
Reserve
NOSTITZ

XXX Advance
Guard
NORDMANN

9.00 p.m.:
Saxon IX Corps
attack Deutsch-
Wagram

Aderklaa   ZEZSCHWITZ DUPAS

Sussenbrunn

POLENZ
BROUSSIER
FONTANELLI SAHUC
LAMARQUE SERRAS THARREAU
PACTHOD
CARCOMBED
FREIRE GRANDJEAN
COLBERT

DURETTE

Baumersdorf

Tower

Stipsicz
Hussars

XXX IV
ROSENBERG

PROVENCHERES

Ober Siebenbrunn

XXX IX
BERNADOTTE

GUTSCHMIDT

LEGRAND

Markgrafneusiedl

Grosshofen

About 8.30 p.m.:
III Corps commences
attack against
Markgrafneusiedl

3.30 p.m.:
Elements of Saxon IX
Corps and Austrian
Advance Guard clash
at Raasdorf

BARRA ST. CYR

Breitenlee

Neu
Wirtshaus

Raasdorf

Young
Guard
Old Guard

ST. GERMAIN

NANSOUTY

ARRIGHI

PUTHOD

GUDIN

FRIANT
MONTBRUN

Glinzendorf

MORAND
GROUCHY

PULLY

Russbach Stream

WALTHER

Esslinger Hof

XXX VI
KLENAU

Pysdorf
XXXX
Army of
Italy
EUGENE

XXX II
OUDINOT

XXX III
DAVOUT

7.00 p.m.:
II Corps and Army
of Italy Commence
attack against
escarpment

Leopoldsdorf

XXX Advance
Guard
NORDMANN

Aspern

Essling

Gross Enzersdorf

2.00 p.m.:
French Army
begins advance
across Marchfeld

Rutzendorf

4 July 9.00 p.m.:
French Army begin to
cross to the Marchfeld

5.00 a.m.:
French IV Corps attack
Gross Enzersdorf

Kimmerleindorf

Lobau

XXX XI
MARMONT   CLAPAREDE CLAUZEL

Ober
Mit-Hausen

Wittau

XXX VII
WREDE   MINUCCI BECKERS
         PREYSING

Muhlleuten

Sachsengang

Danube

N

| 0 | | 1 | | 2 | | 3 Miles |
| 0 | 1 | 2 | 3 | 4 | 5 Km |

◀ *The view from the Austrian position on the escarpment to the right of Baumersdorf looking towards the tree-lined Russbach stream. In this general area Dupas and Macdonald led their attack against Bellegarde's I Korps.*

◀ *The attack by Dupas and Macdonald pushed back the Austrian line. Then, hit by cavalry, Bellegarde was about to give way when Charles arrived and counter-attacked with IR42. This illustration incorrectly depicts the Austrian regiment wearing the later issue shako, and their opponents appear to be Saxons in the 1810 uniform. (HGM, Vienna).*

leadership and rallied his broken first-line troops and re-formed them against the flank of the French, who provided an excellent target, silhouetted against the setting sun. Lamarque's men fell back but were reinforced by Valentin's brigade and Sahuc's cavalry. The cavalry hit the Austrian infantry, but, just as it was about to give way, Charles rode up, inspired the men amid the confusion and led a counter-attack by IR42 (Erbach) against the French infantry. Hohenzollern, having secured his own position, came over to I Korps with the Vincent Chevauxlegers and Hessen-Homberg Hussars and fought off Sahuc's men. With this rapid change of circumstances, the

Frenchmen broke, and in the gathering gloom they mistook Dupas' two white-coated Saxon battalions on their left for Austrians and opened fire. The units, Schützen Bataillon (von Metzsch) and Grenadier Bataillon (von Radeloff), disintegrated, some seeking shelter in the buildings on the edge of Wagram, others fleeing to the rear in disorder. The casualty rate was high. The counter-attack was a complete success, although Charles received a slight wound in the shoulder during the fighting. The reduced quality of the French infantry was noticeable as the retreat became a rout, the fleeing men only halting at Raasdorf when confronted by the Imperial Guard.

▶ *With the battle on the escarpment continuing, Hohenzollern, having secured his own position, led his cavalry to Bellegarde's assistance, driving off the French horsemen. As the sun set, the French infantry broke and were driven off the ridge. (HGM, Vienna).*

The Attack on Deutsch-Wagram

Bernadotte delayed the attack of IX Corps, awaiting the arrival of GL Zezschwitz's division. At about 9.00 p.m. Lecoq's brigade advanced against the village of Wagram, the three Saxon battalions being greeted by heavy musketry from two battalions of IR17 (Reuss-Plauen) and 2tes Jäger, as they emerged from the gloom of the Marchfeld into the light from the burning buildings. Forcing their way in, the Saxons were halted by a third battalion of IR17 in front of the church, whose close-range volleys forced them to seek shelter in the adjoining buildings. As the attack broke down, Zeschau's brigade with Prinz Maximilian's regiment attached were pushed into the confusion to tip the balance; but, disordered in crossing the Russbach and losing any remaining cohesion on entering the smoke-filled, casualty-strewn streets, they too became absorbed by the chaos that reigned in Wagram. The situation in the village was desperate. With the darkness and smoke limiting visibility, with all combatants except the Jäger wearing white uniforms and with almost everybody shouting and calling in German, there were numerous instances of Saxons being fired on by their own countrymen. At about 10.30 p.m. GM Hartitzsch arrived with the last of the Saxon infantry, whereupon he was ordered to advance with the Leib Grenadier Garde battalion, Grenadier Bataillon (von Bose) and Schützen Bataillon (von Egidy) and take Wagram. Unfortunately he was not informed that Saxon troops were already fighting in the village, and as Hartitzsch advanced, numbers of white-coated soldiers emerged from Wagram. Presuming them to be Austrians, his men opened fire, cutting down many of the figures, and it was some minutes before the mistake was realized. For the hard-pressed Saxons in the village this was the last straw. Believing themselves attacked in the rear as well as by fresh Austrian troops in front, they fled from the nightmare village and in disorder fell back on Aderklaa about 11.00 p.m. with only heavy casualties to show for their fruitless endeavours.

On the right, Davout had also attacked late, ordering Morand's and Friant's divisions to cross the Russbach and attack Markgrafneusiedl from the east while Gudin's and Puthod's divisions were to attack the village through Grosshofen. A cavalry probe to the right was thwarted by Nostitz's cavalry division, and the infantry attack soon petered out, leaving the artillery alone to continue with its exchange of fire.

The Night of 5/6 July

All along the line the soldiers of both sides made their fires and settled down for the night to grasp what rest they could, while Napoleon contemplated the failure of his attempt at a quick breakthrough. Reinforcements now became available with the arrival of Marmont's XI Corps and Wrede's Bavarian division, which would enable Napoleon to deploy 140,500 infantry, 28,000 cavalry, 13,500 artillery, engineers, etc. and 488 guns on the Marchfeld, with another 8,500 men and 129 guns in reserve on Lobau. Charles could muster 113,500 infantry, 14,600 cavalry, 9,600 artillery, engineers, etc. and 414 guns. Now knowing the strength of the Austrian position and their resolve to fight, Napoleon felt confident that he could gain a victory. To strengthen his attack even further he ordered Massena to bring the majority of IV Corps north towards Aderklaa at 2.00 a.m. on 6 July, leaving only Boudet's division to cover the approach to his rear. The main thrust of his attack was to be carried out by Davout on the right, turning the flank at Markgrafneusiedl and rolling up the Austrian line while his other corps held them in place.

At Charles' headquarters in Wagram there was also much activity. Although exhausted and weakened by his wound, Charles had been delighted by the performance of his army, and as yet a large part had still to be committed. Aware of Napoleon's superiority in numbers, he felt unable to withstand another major attack. But he also knew of the weakness of Napoleon's left. He was later to write: 'I had decided to seize the only means which could give any prospect of success against the superior enemy, namely to fall on them by surprise on all sides as day broke.' At midnight the orders were issued for a general attack to commence at 4.00 a.m. on 6 July. On the right, VI Korps were to advance on Aspern; to their left, III Korps were instructed to march through Leopoldau towards Breitenlee, keeping in line with the Grenadier Reserve that was to march through Süssenbrunn. The Reserve Cavalry were to move between Süssenbrunn and Aderklaa with I Korps on their left, wheeling out of Wagram and advancing along the Russbach. On the heights, II Korps were to hold their position until I Korps had passed, when they would follow on. On the left, IV Korps, now including the Advance Guard, were to move against Davout and be supported by the arrival of Archduke John with 13,000 men. Watching the Danube and protecting the roads to Bohemia and Moravia, should retreat be necessary, was V Korps.

For the plan to work, coordination of the corps movements was of critical importance, something that the command and control system of the Habsburg army had often struggled to achieve. The

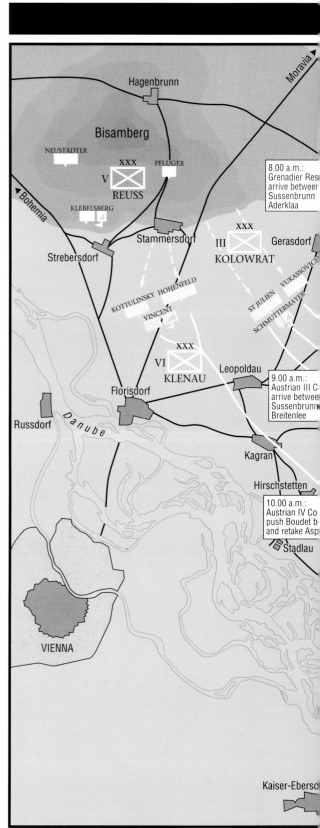

Wagram, 5-6 July 1809: Day Two, 4 a.m. to 10 a.m.

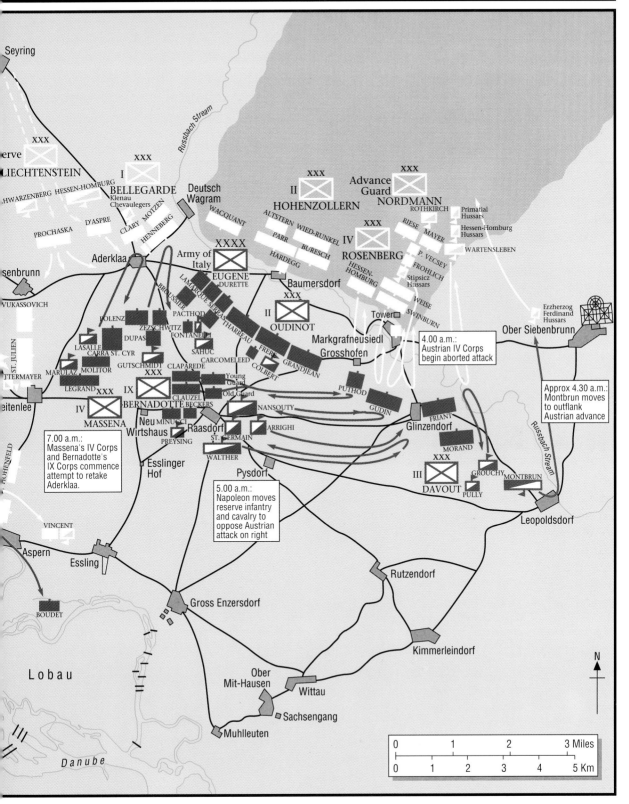

Seyring

XXX
erve
LIECHTENSTEIN

HWARZENBERG HESSEN-HOMBURG

XXX
I
BELLEGARDE
Klenau
Chevaulegers

Deutsch
Wagram

XXX
II
HOHENZOLLERN

Advance
Guard

XXX
NORDMANN
ROTHKIRCH

Primatial
Hussars

Hessen-Homburg
Hussars

PROCHASKA

D'ASPRE

CLARY MOTZEN

HENNEBERG

WACQUANT

ALTSTERN WIED-RUNKEL

XXX
IV
ROSENBERG

RIESE   MAYER

WARTENSLEBEN

Aderklaa

senbrunn

VUKASSOVICH

Army of
Italy

XXXX
EUGENE
DURETTE

PARR   BURESCH

HARDEGG

HESSEN-
HOMBURG

P. VECSEY

FROHLICH

Stipsicz
Hussars

Baumersdorf

LAMARQUE SERAS THARREAU

XXX
II
OUDINOT

Tower

Markgrafneusiedl
Grosshofen

WEISE

SIVINBURN

Erzherzog
Ferdinand
Hussars

Ober Siebenbrunn

ST. JULIEN

TTERMAYER

POLENZ

BROUSSIER

PACTHOD

ZEZSCHWITZ

DUPAS

FONTANELLI

LASALLE

CARRA ST. CYR

GUTSCHMIDT

SAHUC

CARCOMELEED

CLAPAREDE

FRERE

COLBERT

GRANDJEAN

4.00 a.m.:
Austrian IV Corps
begin aborted attack

Approx 4.30 a.m.:
Montbrun moves
to outflank
Austrian advance

MARULAZ

MOLITOR

LEGRAND

XXX
IX
BERNADOTTE

XXX

Young
Guard

Old Guard

CLAUZEL

BECKERS

NANSOUTY

PUTHOD

GUDIN

FRIANT

Glinzendorf

eitenlee

XXX
IV
MASSENA

Neu
Wirtshaus

MINUCCI

Raasdorf

PREYSING

ST. GERMAIN

ARRIGHI

MORAND

XXX
III
DAVOUT

GROUCHY

PULLY

MONTBRUN

7.00 a.m.:
Massena's IV Corps
and Bernadotte's
IX Corps commence
attempt to retake
Aderklaa.

Esslinger
Hof

Pysdorf

WALTHER

5.00 a.m.:
Napoleon moves
reserve infantry
and cavalry to
oppose Austrian
attack on right

Leopoldsdorf

VINCENT

HOHENFELD

Aspern

Essling

Gross Enzersdorf

BOUDET

Rutzendorf

Kimmerleindorf

L o b a u

Ober
Mit-Hausen

Wittau

Sachsengang

Muhlleuten

N

D a n u b e

0		1		2		3 Miles
0	1	2	3	4		5 Km

two corps farthest from headquarters, VI and III Korps, were also farthest from the French. To be in position for the attack by 4.00 a.m. they needed to commence their march at 1.00 a.m., but they were not to receive their orders until 3.00 a.m. Meanwhile, Charles expected news of the arrival of Archduke John at any moment – in fact, his brother was still in Pressburg and did not commence his 40-kilometre march until 1.00 a.m.

6 July 1809: The Second Day

At 4.00 a.m., in accordance with his orders, Rosenberg on the Austrian left formed his men into three great columns and sent them against Davout. The brigade of Hessen-Homburg advanced with six battalions against Grosshofen; the second column, with twelve line battalions and four of Landwehr, from Swinburn's and Weiss' brigades moved on Glinzendorf, both columns preceded by an advanced guard of ten battalions commanded by FML Radetzky and supported by the Stipsicz Hussars. To the left of the infantry, a cavalry column of 30 squadrons commanded by FML Nostitz, drawn from the Advance Guard and Wartensleben's brigade, aimed to outflank the French, while the Erzherzog Ferdinand Hussars rode to Ober Siebenbrunn to protect their flank.

Taking them by surprise, as planned, Radetzky drove back Davout's outposts. From Grosshofen, Puthod's division opened fire on the slowly approaching Austrians, as did Friant's and Gudin's divisions from Glinzendorf, while Grouchy's dragoons rode to oppose the cavalry column. Montbrun sent part of his light cavalry towards Ober Siebenbrunn to outflank the Austrian move in that direction. At French headquarters in Raasdorf the sound of firing convinced Napoleon that Archduke John had appeared with a force he believed to number 30,000 men; to protect his threatened right he ordered Nansouty and Arrighi's cuirassier divisions to support Davout and started out himself with his reserve infantry, the Imperial Guard and Marmont's XI Corps.

Charles now became concerned. Although IV Korps had started their advance on time, there was no sign of III or VI Korps far away on the right. Unwilling to expose Rosenberg's men to the full might of the French army unsupported, he issued orders for IV Korps to extricate itself from its now isolated position and return to its starting line. The aborted attack cost IV Korps many lives. And now realizing the attack had not heralded the arrival of Archduke John, Napoleon issued orders to Eugène and Oudinot to pin the Austrian line on the Russbach while Davout prepared to unleash his attack on Markgrafneusiedl. Then, leaving Arrighi

◄ *Following the Saxons' abandonment of Aderklaa, the village was occupied by Bellegarde's I Korps. Massena was ordered to recapture it immediatly, and St. Cyr's division was selected for the task. The illustration depicts the 4e Ligne storming through the village and driving the defenders from the buildings. (Musée de l'Armée, Paris).*

with Davout, he returned with his reserve to Raasdorf.

The French Attack on Aderklaa

Back at headquarters, Napoleon was immediately faced with a new threat. In the early hours of the morning, without orders, Bernadotte had withdrawn his shaken IX Corps from their exposed position at Aderklaa to a safer one south-east of the village. Just after 3.00 a.m. Bellegarde had tentatively advanced towards Aderklaa with I Korps, expecting to encounter strong resistance. Instead his advance guard reported the village undefended. Delighted with his good fortune, Bellegarde immediately occupied Aderklaa, and the space between it and Wagram, with the brigades of Henneberg, Clary, Motzen and Stutterheim, deployed in two lines. An exchange of artillery fire opened up with the Saxons, which, when joined by the artillery of II Korps on the Wagram, caused many casualties on both sides. Massena, who had been ordered towards Aderklaa with IV Corps during the night, now arrived and was immediately detailed to recapture the village by Napoleon, who was furious with Bernadotte for abandoning it.

The attack was entrusted to St. Cyr's division, led by 24ème Légère and 4ème Ligne, supported by the Hessian brigade, with 46ème in reserve. On their right, the Saxons were to attack between Aderklaa and Wagram. Urged forward with impatience by Massena from a carriage (he had been injured a few days before), St. Cyr's men swept forward into a hail of bullets, undaunted by the casualties that fell all around. The defenders of the village lost heart and broke, streaming back on to their second line. But, inspired by Bellegarde, the second line held firm, and the fugitives re-formed. The French, who had pursued through the village, emerged and came face to face with an overwhelming mass of close-range musketry. All along the line the attackers were hit hard. Unable to hold on in the face of such fire, both French and German troops ran to the rear, a number seeking shelter in Aderklaa. On the right, as the Saxons had begun to withdraw, they were attacked by light cavalry, and the panic this induced sent a large percentage in flight towards Raasdorf, where only the personal intervention of Napoleon halted them. A stiff exchange of words with their commander, Bernadotte, followed.

At the same time, the first of the grenadier battalions of the reserve were coming into position to the right of I Korps. Eager to press the French back, GM Stutterheim led the first three of these battalions, those of Scovaud, Jambline and Brzeczinski, plus two battalions of IR42 (Erbach) against the village, capturing it after a period of

▶ *Following Massena's capture of Aderklaa, the Austrians attempted to retake the village with the first elements of the Grenadier Reserve, which had just arrived, and two battalions of IR42. This illustration shows IR42 smashing into the French troops, who were forced to release their grip on the village after much intense fighting. (Bibliothèque des Arts Decoratifs, Paris, Collection Maciet).*

intense and bloody hand-to-hand combat. Un-deterred, Massena launched the light cavalry of Lasalle and Marulaz against the Austrian batteries that drew up in front of the village, scattering the gunners; but the presence of Liechtenstein's cavalry forced the French to abandon the guns they had captured. Massena thereupon organized another infantry attack, throwing Molitor's division against the increasingly secure position. Five battalion's of Leguay's brigade and the 67ème Ligne from Viviez's stormed through the killing ground in front of Aderklaa, taking severe casualties, before entering and regaining control briefly before fresh Austrian grenadier battalions arrived and ejected them in disorder, Legrand's division covering their retreat.

At 9.00 a.m., Charles was in a strong position. I Korps had achieved its objective, forming between Wagram and Aderklaa, while the Grenadier Reserve was extending the line towards Süssenbrunn. On the French side, Eugène had been forced to face Macdonald's men westwards to protect his flank following the retreat of the Saxons, and Massena was busy reforming his men after two murderous assaults on Aderklaa. This would have been the ideal time for I Korps and the Grenadier Reserve, supported by the Reserve Cavalry, to have advanced against Napoleon's weakened left. But for the corps commanders this was not possible. Their orders had been clear: each corps was to align its forward movement on the corps to its left and right. The great distance to be covered by III Korps meant they were only just coming into view, beginning to move up into line with their left on the Grenadier Reserve at Süssenbrunn and their right on the village of Breitenlee.

Although concerned by the imminent arrival of III Korps, Napoleon was more worried by the growing cloud of dust beyond them, which signified the advance of VI Korps. Although they had begun their march late, the route ahead of them into Napoleon's rear was barred only by Boudet's single division of IV Corps.

Napoleon's Crisis

Klenau, who had held command of VI Korps for only two days, pushed on as quickly as he could

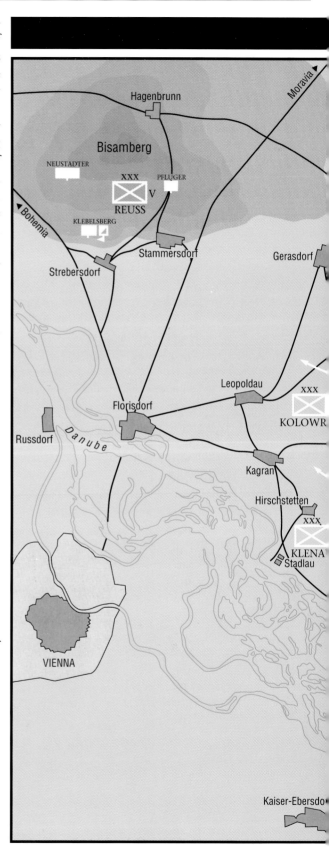

Wagram, 5-6 July 1809: Day Two, 10 a.m. to 3 p.m.

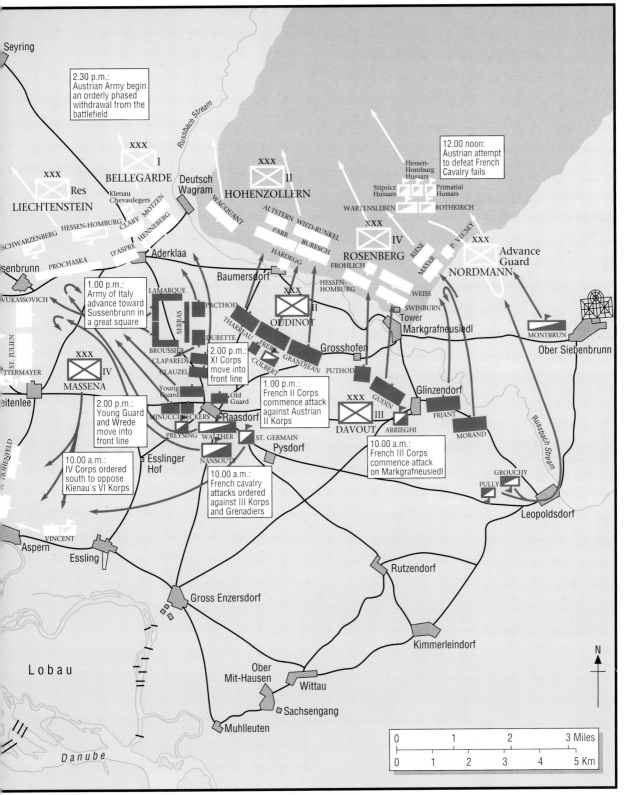

Seyring

2.30 p.m.:
Austrian Army begin an orderly phased withdrawal from the battlefield

Russbach Stream

XXX
I
BELLEGARDE
Deutsch Wagram

XXX
II
HOHENZOLLERN

XXX
Res
LIECHTENSTEIN

XXX

Klenau Chevaulegers

SCHWARZENBERG
HESSEN-HOMBURG
CLARY
MOTZEN
HENNEBERG
D'ASPRE
PROCHASKA

senbrunn

VUKASSOVICH

ST. JULIEN

TTERMAYER

XXX
IV
MASSENA

eitenlee

HOHENFELD

Aderklaa

Baumersdorf

HARDEGG

WACQUANT

ALTSTERN
WIED-RUNKEL

PARR
BURESCH

Hessen-Homburg Hussars

Stipsicz Hussars
Primatial Hussars

WARTENSLEBEN
ROTHKIRCH

12.00 noon:
Austrian attempt to defeat French Cavalry fails

XXX
IV
ROSENBERG

FROHLICH

RIESE
MAYER

P. VECSEY

XXX
Advance Guard
NORDMANN

HESSEN-HOMBURG

WEISE

SWINBURN
Tower
Markgrafneusiedl

MONTBRUN

Ober Siebenbrunn

1.00 p.m.:
Army of Italy advance toward Sussenbrunn in a great square

LAMARQUE

PACTHOD

SERRAS

THARREAU
DURETTE

BROUSSIER
CLAPAREDE
CLAUZEL

Young Guard

MINUCCI BECKERS

PREYSING
WALTHER

NANSOUTY

Esslinger Hof

2.00 p.m.:
Young Guard and Wrede move into front line

10.00 a.m.:
IV Corps ordered south to oppose Klenau's VI Korps

FRERE
COLBERT

GRANDJEAN

XXX
II
OUDINOT

2.00 p.m.:
XI Corps move into front line

Old Guard

Raasdorf

ST. GERMAIN

Pysdorf

10.00 a.m.:
French cavalry attacks ordered against III Korps and Grenadiers

Grosshofen

PUTHOD

1.00 p.m.:
French II Corps commence attack against Austrian II Korps

XXX
III
DAVOUT

GUDIN

ARRIEGHI

Glinzendorf

FRIANT

MORAND

10.00 a.m.:
French III Corps commence attack on Markgrafneusiedl

Russbach Stream

GROUCHY
PULLY

Leopoldsdorf

Aspern
VINCENT

Essling

Gross Enzersdorf

Rutzendorf

Kimmerleindorf

Lobau

Ober Mit-Hausen

Wittau

Sachsengang

Muhlleuten

Danube

N

0		1		2		3 Miles
0	1	2	3	4		5 Km

▲ Having lost control of Aderklaa, Massena ordered another attempt on the village. Molitor sent seven of his battalions forward, braving furious fire, and regained control. However, they were ejected again when fresh grenadier battalions moved up to attack.

◄ FML Klenau pushed forward towards Aspern with VI Korps, forming the right flank of the Austrian advance and driving Boudet's outposts before him. At Aspern, the Liechtenstein and Kienmayer Hussars captured Boudet's artillery, forcing him to abandon the village and fall back into the Mühlau. (HGM, Vienna).

down the Kagran–Aspern road, driving in Boudet's outposts and overpowering his outnumbered division. An attempt to defend the ruins of Aspern failed, and with his artillery captured by GM Wallmoden's hussar brigade Boudet drew back into the Mühlau. By 10.00 a.m. Klenau had his outposts in Essling, but finding himself ahead of the main infantry line he halted, in accordance with orders, redressed his lines towards Breitenlee and waited for the advance of III Korps. The critical moment of the battle had arrived. Klenau had broken through the French left and had only the unprotected rear of the army ahead of him, about five kilometres away.

From his central position at Raasdorf, Napoleon observed the attack on his left. Since he held the inner line of the curved battlefront, he could use his shorter lines of communication to great advantage. Believing the time was now right, he ordered Davout, who had been preparing for two hours, to launch the attack against Markgrafneusiedl on the right – this, he felt, was the key to victory. Oudinot was to continue to occupy the attention of the Austrian line to his front. Having issued these orders, Napoleon initiated the moves designed to secure his open left flank. Instead of committing his reserve infantry to meet the threat, he instructed Massena to march south with his regrouping IV Corps and block any further advance by Klenau's VI Korps. To execute this order Massena would have to march across the face of the Grenadier Reserve and III Korps – an extremely dangerous manoeuvre. But Napoleon had no intention of exposing this already shaken corps to unnecessary punishment: to shield this move, Bessières was ordered to attack the weakest point in the Austrian line, the junction between the now-advancing III Korps and Grenadier Reserve, with his cavalry. Because of the commitment of d'Aspre's division of the Reserve to the attack on Aderklaa, only Prochaska's division remained to deploy in one line between that village and Süssenbrunn, supported by the Reserve Cavalry.

The cavalry attack was not well handled. The Guard Cavalry appear not to have received the order. St. Germain's division were held in reserve and not committed, leaving Nansouty's division of cuirassiers and carabiniers to face the brunt of the fighting. About 4,000 metal-clad horsemen advanced towards the Austrian line between Süssenbrunn and Aderklaa, drawing a devastating fire upon themselves; casualties mounted so quickly that only Defranc's carabinier brigade reached the enemy, where, confronted by the infantry drawn up in masses and Hessen-Homberg's cuirassier division, they could do nothing but turn and ride back, again running the gauntlet of Austrian fire. Bessières was wounded in this attack. The Guard Cavalry, too late to support the attack, stirred into

▶ *To protect Massena's redeployment as he marched across the face of the Austrian line, Napoleon ordered the heavy cavalry to attack the junction between the Grenadier Reserve and III Korps. The attack exposed Nansouty's men to heavy casulties as they charged into a hail of musketry and cannon fire, forcing them to retire.*

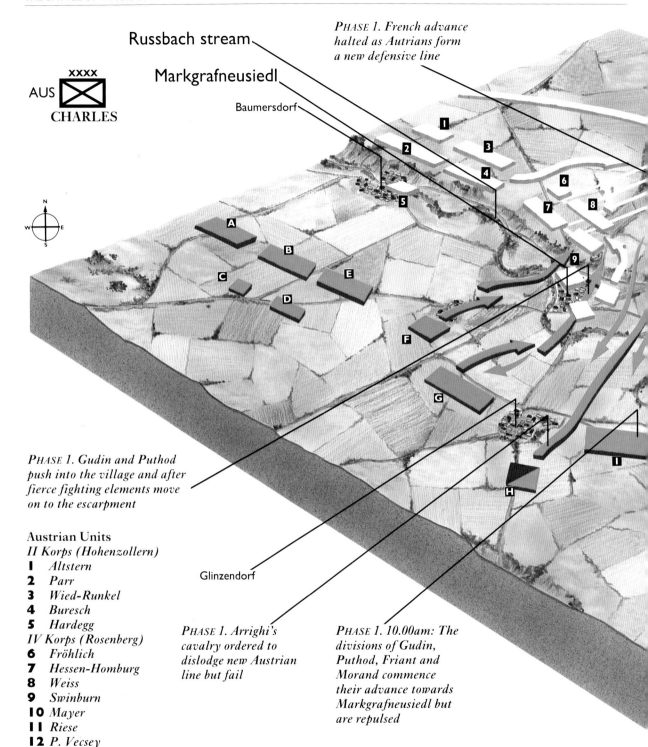

Russbach stream

Markgrafneusiedl

Baumersdorf

PHASE 1. French advance halted as Autrians form a new defensive line

AUS **CHARLES** xxxx

A B C D E F G H I

1 2 3 4 5 6 7 8 9

PHASE 1. Gudin and Puthod push into the village and after fierce fighting elements move on to the escarpment

Glinzendorf

Austrian Units
II Korps (Hohenzollern)
1 *Altstern*
2 *Parr*
3 *Wied-Runkel*
4 *Buresch*
5 *Hardegg*
IV Korps (Rosenberg)
6 *Fröhlich*
7 *Hessen-Homburg*
8 *Weiss*
9 *Swinburn*
10 *Mayer*
11 *Riese*
12 *P. Vecsey*
13 *Nostitz*

PHASE 1. Arrighi's cavalry ordered to dislodge new Austrian line but fail

PHASE 1. 10.00am: The divisions of Gudin, Puthod, Friant and Morand commence their advance towards Markgrafneusiedl but are repulsed

THE BATTLE OF WAGRAM, 6 JULY 1809

Davout's attack on Markgrafneusiedl, 10.00am–1.00pm

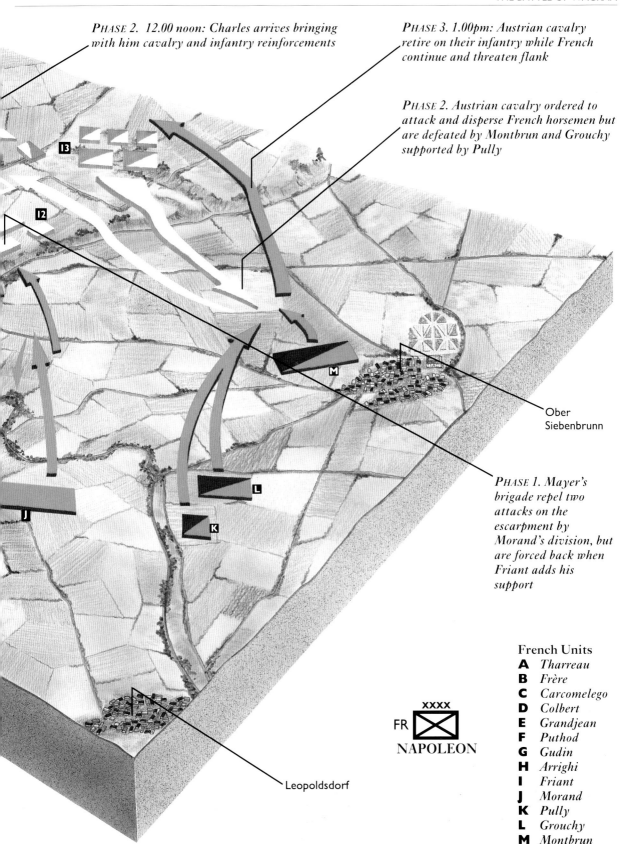

PHASE 2. 12.00 noon: Charles arrives bringing with him cavalry and infantry reinforcements

PHASE 3. 1.00pm: Austrian cavalry retire on their infantry while French continue and threaten flank

PHASE 2. Austrian cavalry ordered to attack and disperse French horsemen but are defeated by Montbrun and Grouchy supported by Pully

Ober Siebenbrunn

PHASE 1. Mayer's brigade repel two attacks on the escarpment by Morand's division, but are forced back when Friant adds his support

Leopoldsdorf

FR ⊠ XXXX
NAPOLEON

French Units
A	*Tharreau*
B	*Frère*
C	*Carcomelego*
D	*Colbert*
E	*Grandjean*
F	*Puthod*
G	*Gudin*
H	*Arrighi*
I	*Friant*
J	*Morand*
K	*Pully*
L	*Grouchy*
M	*Montbrun*

action and charged the line themselves, but the Chasseurs à cheval and Polish chevauxlegers failed to achieve a breakthrough.

Although costly, these attacks succeeded in halting the Austrian advance, and Massena commenced his move south. While the cavalry attack was under way, Napoleon issued orders for the second part of his plan to protect Massena's march. A great artillery battery was to be formed in an arc to cover the ground between Aderklaa and Breitenlee. Under Général Lauriston of the Guard Artillery, 112 guns, drawn from the Guard, the Army of Italy and Wrede's Bavarians, soon unleashed such a weight of iron against the Austrians that great holes were torn through their lines, twisted bodies being flung high in the air and whole files disappearing as a great evil-smelling cloud of smoke engulfed the scene gradually masking the horror. The burning corn around the battery, set alight by sparks and discarded match

from the guns, soon swallowed up the wounded all around who were unable to crawl from its path. Kolowrat, unable to advance into the barrage with III Korps, ordered his men to retire to the Breitenlee–Süssenbrunn road. Once out of canister range, he unlimbered his own artillery and opened a counter-battery fire as he observed Massena marching past his corps. Although receiving some artillery fire, Massena was beyond the reach of Kolowrat's muskets and able to continue his march

in relative safety thanks to the combined efforts of the cavalry and artillery. By noon he had arrived close to Aspern and, supported by Lasalle's light cavalry, St. Germain's cuirassier brigade and the artillery based on Lobau, he began to engage Klenau and VI Korps, who were still waiting to advance. Reassured that his left was now secure, Napoleon ordered Macdonald to deploy his two divisions of the Army of Italy behind the Grand Battery, with Serras' division, to be ready to exploit any opportunities presented by the success of the artillery.

Davout Storms Markgrafneusiedl

While the fate of the battle had swung in the balance on the French left, on their right Davout's careful preparations were about to bring reward. A destructive bombardment had been continuing against Markgrafneusiedl for some time. The village was the keystone of the Austrian left, its houses and church lying between the Russbach and the Wagram, overlooked by an old disused church topped by a square stone tower. The effect of the bombardment had been terrible for the defenders: most of their artillery was out of action, and fires that had started in some of the buildings were quickly spreading.

At 10.00 a.m. Davout launched his attack. To the east of Markgrafneusiedl the cavalry divisions of Montbrun, Grouchy and Pully drove off the hussars commanded by Frölich at Ober Siebenbrunn and continued their advance, threatening to turn the Austrian left flank. To oppose this move, Rosenberg ordered Mayer's brigade to form a new flank on the escarpment where it turns to the north-east; Riese's brigade, joined by IR58 (Beaulieu), drew up behind them. On the extreme left, Rosenberg massed his cavalry, which included FML Nostitz's division

◀ *Napoleon's crisis. From his position north of Raasdorf, Napoleon (right foreground) has ordered Massena (left centre) to oppose the Austrian VI Korps at Aspern. French cavalry move towards the* *Austrian line (centre) while artillery (left foreground) move to form the Grand Battery. Macdonald begins to form his square (right centre). (Musée de l'Armée, Paris).*

◄ *A modern photograph of the tower at Markgraf-neusiedl. At the time of the battle the tower was square, the building itself having served as a church and watch-tower. It had been abandoned for some time, as a new church had been built in the village below. The square tower was replaced by a round one when it was later converted for use as a windmill.*

from the reserve, a total of 38½ squadrons. Around the tower were the brigades of Weiss, Hessen-Homburg and Swinburn, with two additional battalions.

As Davout's infantry began to advance, many anxious Austrian eyes scanned the eastern horizon searching for a sign of the approach of Archduke John – to no avail. The divisions of Gudin and Puthod stormed forward against the front of the village to be greeted by a withering fire from the defenders, which induced hesitation in their ranks. To the east of the village, Morand's and Friant's divisions moved forward to receive a similar greeting combined with cavalry attacks. Further attacks by the four divisions rolled forward only to shudder to a halt, pull back a little, re-form and

► *Major of the French 8ème Hussars. As part of Laselle's light cavalry division the 8ème (Piré's brigade) were heavily involved in the fighting at Aspern-Essling throughout both days of the battle. At Wagram, with IV Corps, they were involved in the attacks around Aderklaa. (Angus McBride)*

◄ *Davout's horse is shot under him as III Corps launch their attack towards the tower above the village of Markgraf-neusiedl. Fierce fighting continues in the streets of the village below the escarpment in the background. (Anne S. K. Brown Collection).*

◄ Overcoming a fierce defence, Gudin's and Puthod's divisions of III Corps entered the burning village of Markgraf-neusiedl, where their attacks dissolved into a series of ferocious running battles through the streets. Part of IR49 (Kerpen), in the foreground, are shown attempting to halt the French advance.

attack again. In these brief periods of respite, Austrian casualties limped or were carried away to medical stations set up in the houses at the rear of the burning village. The situation in Markgraf-neusiedl was itself becoming desperate, for fire was quickly spreading through the village. The exhausted defenders, already oppressed by the heat of the day, must have felt as though they were trapped in a hellish inferno, a feeling heightened by the unearthly screams of the wounded as they burnt to death, unable to escape the smoke-filled buildings where they lay.

At this point a renewed assault by Gudin and Puthod reached the village, forcing Rohan's men to give ground, vicious fighting continuing through the houses with a part of the French force penetrating as far as the tower. Hessen-Homburg's brigade pulled back a little and formed a new line to oppose the French foothold on the escarpment. Fighting flowed back and forth around the tower, while to the east the assault continued. Morand's men had reached the escarpment but were repulsed

► East of Markgraf-neusiedl, Morand's division of III Corps stormed the escarpment but were repulsed twice by Mayer's brigade of the Advance Guard. A third assault, illustrated here, led by 30e Ligne, proved successful, and Mayer's men were forced to fall back on Riese's brigade. (Musée de l'Armée, Paris).

by Mayer's brigade, a second effort meeting the same fate; but at the same time senior casualties were mounting in the Austrian lines, these including FML Nordmann, commanding the Advance Guard. The next assault by Morand, supported by Friant, was too much for Mayer's brigade, who gave way and fell back on Riese's men, where they reformed. Friant's attempt to hold this position on the escarpment was at first thwarted, but a second effort saw his men pushing in on the tower from the east.

Unable to retake the tower with the Hessen-Homburg brigade, and having lost his grip on Markgrafneusiedl, where fighting had been as fierce as any yet encountered during the campaign, Rosenberg pulled back and formed a new line,

which halted any further French advance. In an effort to dislodge this line, Davout ordered Arrighi to charge the position with his cuirassier division. Despite his protests, Arrighi was obliged to carry out the attack across the most unlikely cavalry ground and the attack failed.

At about noon, with the Austrians now evicted from Markgrafneusiedl, Charles, who had observed the danger developing on his left, rode over from Wagram with Buresch's brigade from II Korps and the Hohenzollern Cuirassiers from the Reserve. Forming up the newly arrived cavalry with that of Nostitz, Charles ordered it to defeat the cavalry of Montbrun and Grouchy before attacking the exposed French infantry. Meanwhile, Davout was

ordering a similar move. The resulting cavalry clash occurred north-east of Markgrafneusiedl. About 30 Austrian squadrons attacked about 9 of Montbrun's. Heavily outnumbered, the French initially gave way, but gradually more French squadrons were fed in until the advance of Grouchy's dragoon division tipped the balance, the much disordered Austrian cavalry retiring on their infantry. It was now about 1.00 p.m. Both Charles and Napoleon recognized that the end of the battle was in sight.

The Destruction of Macdonald's Square

In his central position, observing from afar the signs of Davout's progress, Napoleon began issuing orders for a general assault all along the line. Massena was to attack Klenau vigorously around Aspern; Oudinot with II Corps was to storm the escarpment and dislodge Hohenzollern's II Korps; while in the French centre Macdonald was to lead a massed attack against III Korps and the Grenadier Reserve. Although his force amounted to 30 battalions, these had been much weakened, and there were only about 8,000 men. The formation into which they were organized was unusual – a great square, each side made up of battalions arranged in column of divisions, two companies across by three companies deep. The front of the square was made up of eight battalions, a regiment

▲ *GD Macdonald was born in France, the son of a Scots Jacobite exile. He began his military career in 1784, aged 19, serving under Dumouriez and Pichegru. In 1799 he commanded the Army of Naples but fell from grace with Napoleon in 1804. In 1809, Macdonald was re-establishing his position, commanding a corps in the Army of Italy. (HGM, Vienna).*

drawn from both Broussier's and Lamarque's divisions. The right of this great square was to be protected by the Guard Cavalry, while Nansouty's division was to cover the left, and the Grand Battery was to advance to the right and open a heavy fire on the Austrian line.

As these guns moved forward, the Austrian gunners opened an accurate and devastating fire that disabled fifteen of the French pieces before they had completed their move, and the Austrian line then drew back out of canister range again. At about 1.00 p.m. Macdonald's lumbering juggernaut of a formation edged towards the waiting Austrians, who, presented with such a large, slow-moving target, opened up with all they could bring to bear. The destruction within the square was horrific. The

▲ *The attack of Macdonald's square. The square moved slowly across the cornfields of the Marchfeld, heading towards the village of Sussenbrunn. The* *devastating fire of the Austrian Grenadier Reserve and III Korps, brought to bear on this dense target, caused massive casualties. (Romain Baulesch)*

French cavalry launched repeated attacks against the flanks of III Korps and the Grenadier Reserve but had little success. Throughout this, the square continued to move forward against the space between the two corps, aiming for the church spire in Süssenbrunn. Whether due to pressure from the cavalry or from the square itself, the right of the Grenadiers and the left of III Korps pulled back a little. Unable to manoeuvre effectively, the square was drawn into this space so that it came under assault from three sides by close-range musketry. Within one hour of Macdonald's 8,000 men commencing the advance, barely 1,500 remained on their feet.

However, the developing situation on their left and right meant that the Austrians were unable to

◀ *Macdonald's huge attack square was assailed on all sides by artillery and musketry, causing terrible casulties, but the limited Austrian cavalry attacks had little* *effect. The illustration here shows the 106e Ligne of Seras' division repulsing an attack by Schwarzenberg's cavalry. (Musée de l'Armée, Paris).*

exploit the destruction of Macdonald's formation. While Davout on the right had gained control of Markgrafneusiedl, on the left Massena's revitalized IV Corps had begun to exert pressure on Klenau, who by 2.00 p.m., with his outposts already recalled from Essling, was forced out of Aspern, gradually falling back before the French advance.

To relieve the pressure that was crushing Macdonald, Napoleon ordered Pacthod's reserve division of the Army of Italy to launch an attack towards Wagram, while Marmont moved forward to fill the gap now created to the left of Oudinot, and Durutte's division, the last of Eugène's army, was to move to Macdonald's left and storm Breitenlee. To the direct assistance of Macdonald, Napoleon sent Wrede's Bavarian division, which moved to the right of the shattered square, supported by the Young Guard. Napoleon had now committed all but the two regiments of Old Guard.

The End in Sight

Charles, on the heights above the Russbach, with his army outnumbered, knew the battle had turned

▲ Bavarian infantry in pursuit of the Austrian line following Charles's decision to begin a phased withdrawal. Austrian artillery and cavalry attempt to protect the retiring infantry. (Musée de l'Armée, Paris).

▶ A Chevauxlegers Polonais presents Napoleon with a captured Austrian infantry standard. Although the Austrians were defeated, they captured slightly more trophies than the French, provoking Napoleon's comment, 'War was never like this, neither prisoners nor guns. This day will have no result.' (Musée de l'Armée).

against him. His three corps (I, II and IV) that had started the battle on the Russbach line had now been in action for ten hours and were exhausted. Rosenberg's IV Korps was being pushed back and in danger of being outflanked by Davout's cavalry. This forward movement by Davout had finally forced the Austrian troops defending Baumersdorf, which they had held since the opening of the battle the previous day, to evacuate the village, as Oudinot's men came forward. Bellegarde's I Korps, after a whole day in action, now faced Marmont's fresh XI Corps, while on the right Klenau was falling back before Massena. At about 2.00 p.m. Charles received word that Archduke John would not reach the battlefield until 5.00 p.m.

Rather than risk the destruction of his army, which alone could secure the future of the Habsburg dynasty, Charles issued orders for a phased withdrawal at about 2.30 p.m. Each corps was directed along its own line of retreat, and repeated French attacks attempting to disrupt this movement were beaten off as the Austrian army, retaining its discipline, organized counter-attacks to relieve this pressure. In one of these rearguard actions the French light cavalry leader, Lasalle, was killed. By nightfall contact had been broken. The French camped, widely distributed across the battlefield, too exhausted to pursue any further.

Some time after 5.00 p.m., Archduke John's cavalry approached Ober Siebenbrunn. Receiving information that the battle was over, he turned and retraced his steps – but not before his appearance had caused a certain amount of panic among the French troops recovering at Glinzendorf. After a

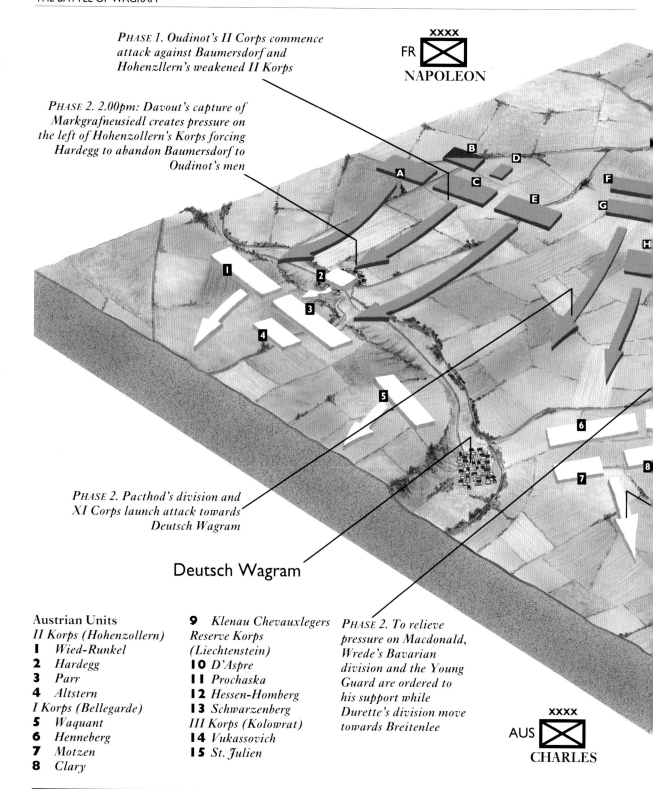

PHASE 1. *Oudinot's II Corps commence attack against Baumersdorf and Hohenzllern's weakened II Korps*

PHASE 2. 2.00pm: *Davout's capture of Markgrafneusiedl creates pressure on the left of Hohenzollern's Korps forcing Hardegg to abandon Baumersdorf to Oudinot's men*

FR NAPOLEON

PHASE 2. *Pacthod's division and XI Corps launch attack towards Deutsch Wagram*

Deutsch Wagram

Austrian Units

II Korps (Hohenzollern)
1 *Wied-Runkel*
2 *Hardegg*
3 *Parr*
4 *Altstern*

I Korps (Bellegarde)
5 *Waquant*
6 *Henneberg*
7 *Motzen*
8 *Clary*

9 *Klenau Chevauxlegers*
Reserve Korps (Liechtenstein)
10 *D'Aspre*
11 *Prochaska*
12 *Hessen-Homberg*
13 *Schwarzenberg*
III Korps (Kolowrat)
14 *Vukassovich*
15 *St. Julien*

PHASE 2. *To relieve pressure on Macdonald, Wrede's Bavarian division and the Young Guard are ordered to his support while Durette's division move towards Breitenlee*

AUS CHARLES

THE BATTLE OF WAGRAM, 6 JULY 1809

Napoleon's attempt to break through the Austrian centre 1.00pm–2.30pm

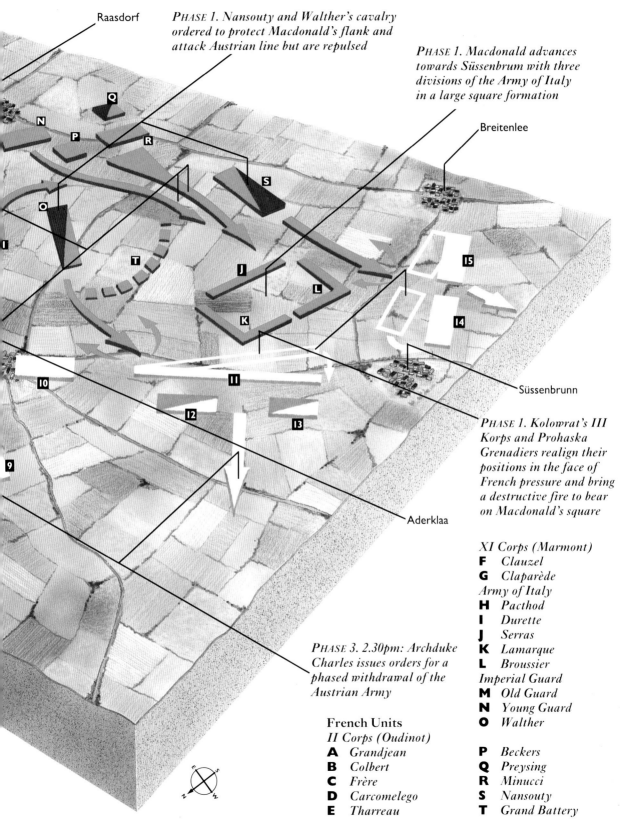

Raasdorf

PHASE 1. Nansouty and Walther's cavalry ordered to protect Macdonald's flank and attack Austrian line but are repulsed

PHASE 1. Macdonald advances towards Süssenbrum with three divisions of the Army of Italy in a large square formation

Breitenlee

Süssenbrunn

PHASE 1. Kolowrat's III Korps and Prohaska Grenadiers realign their positions in the face of French pressure and bring a destructive fire to bear on Macdonald's square

Aderklaa

PHASE 3. 2.30pm: Archduke Charles issues orders for a phased withdrawal of the Austrian Army

French Units
II Corps (Oudinot)
A   *Grandjean*
B   *Colbert*
C   *Frère*
D   *Carcomelego*
E   *Tharreau*

XI Corps (Marmont)
F   *Clauzel*
G   *Claparède*
Army of Italy
H   *Pacthod*
I   *Durette*
J   *Serras*
K   *Lamarque*
L   *Broussier*
Imperial Guard
M   *Old Guard*
N   *Young Guard*
O   *Walther*

P   *Beckers*
Q   *Preysing*
R   *Minucci*
S   *Nansouty*
T   *Grand Battery*

few hours' rest that night, Charles ordered the retreat of his defeated, but still intact, army into Bohemia.

Wagram had been the largest battle in history at that time. More than 300,000 men had fought for two days along a great front. Estimates for the losses sustained by the two sides vary greatly. For the Austrians, a figure of 23,750 killed and wounded, 7,500 prisoners and about 10,000 missing, many of whom returned to their regiments later, seems reasonable. In addition, the Austrians lost ten standards and 20 guns. Estimates of French losses also vary, but 27,500 killed and wounded, with an additional 10,000 for prisoners and missing, seems fair. It is interesting to note that the French lost slightly more trophies than the Austrians, twelve eagles or standards and 21 guns. After the battle, Napoleon was reported as saying that, 'war was never like this, neither prisoners nor guns. This day will have no result.'

▲ The Austrians conducted an orderly retreat. Kolowrat's III Korps fell back to Stammersdorf, where they turned and prepared to attack the French. A French cavalry thrust captured a battery, but the combined efforts of the infantry and cavalry enabled the Schwarzenberg Uhlans to recapture the guns and repulse the French. (HGM, Vienna).

The retreat was well screened by the Austrians and it was a couple of days before Napoleon discovered their exact direction. Numerous rearguard actions led to a further sanguinary encounter around the town of Znaim on 10 July, the fighting in the streets, lasting 36 hours, losing nothing in intensity.

As a stalemate became to appear more obvious, Charles directed Liechtenstein to approach Napoleon with a request for an armistice. While the battle raged, the two men discussed terms, and finally in the late afternoon of 11 July a cease-fire was announced.

▶ *The true cost and horror of war. Interred in the cavernous crypt of the village church in Markgrafneusiedl lies a silent testimony to the fierce and tragic fighting that took place around that village. Here, stacked from floor to ceiling, can be found the bones of those who as enemies fought each other for their lives but in death lie together as one.*

▼ *The Battle of Znaim. The pursuing French caught up with the Austrians on 10 July at Znaim (Znojmo), where another vicious battle developed, lasting almost 36 hours. While the battle was still being fought in earnest, peace negotiations were completed and the campaign of 1809 came to an end. (Anne S. K. Brown Collection).*

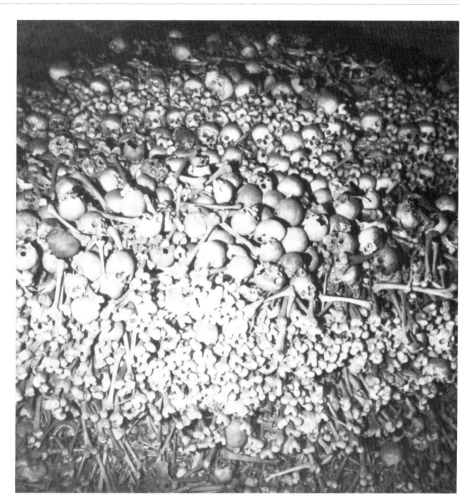

AFTERMATH

Napoleon had been happy to agree to an armistice. He was aware that he could not prevent Charles withdrawing his army from Znaim to the north again. If he were forced to follow he would be moving farther from Vienna, where his communications could be cut by Archduke John and the other commanders that had been operating separately. For his part, Charles had lost the will to fight on and was concerned for the preservation of his exhausted and hungry army. When the emperor, Francis, was informed of the terms of the armistice he was furious, believing Charles had gone beyond his jurisdiction. The long-standing feud between the imperial brothers reached a head. Charles, with his authority curtailed, felt obliged to resign his command on 23 July. Francis believed that the fight could be continued, but Liechtenstein, now commanding the army, advised him that this was no longer practical. The long-awaited British diversionary attack finally materialized during August at Walcheren in Holland, not Germany as expected – not only too late, it was a dismal failure.

The Peace of Schönbrunn was eventually signed after much negotiation in October. It ceded Salzburg and the Inn region to Bavaria, while France took numerous tracts of Habsburg land. New territories were also handed to the Grand Duchy of Warsaw and Russia. In total, the Habsburg empire lost 3,500,000 subjects, was required to pay a heavy financial indemnity and had her army restricted to 150,000 men.

The terms were extremely favourable to France, but it had not been a decisive campaign like those in previous years. Napoleon, guilty of underestimating his enemy, had forgotten one of his own principles of war: 'There is nothing better than to march on to the enemy's capital after a decisive victory; before it, no!' Yet Napoleon did just that. Having failed to crush the Austrian army at Eggmühl, he allowed it to retire largely unmolested while he marched into Vienna for a hollow victory, the ensuing battle of Aspern–Essling resulting in his first personal defeat. The subsequent victory at Wagram demonstrated his own great personal abilities, but again he was unable to inflict a *decisive* defeat on his dogged and determined opponents.

Generous in victory, Napoleon rewarded the roles played by Marmont, Oudinot and Macdonald by installing them as Marshals of the Empire. Bernadotte, however, who had inexplicably claimed much of the honour of the victory for himself and the Saxon Corps, was dismissed from command. Napoleon also revised his contemptuous opinion of the Habsburg army. He had been much impressed with its steadiness and determination, and henceforth anyone denigrating the Austrians in his presence would receive the retort, 'It is obvious you were not at Wagram.' Charles, Austria's best military commander by far, never again held a field command, for the rift between the brothers was now too deep. Having earned Napoleon's respect as a great and able opponent, he was to remain in virtual retirement until his death in 1847.

For the rest of Europe, Austria had broken the spell of Napoleon's invincibility. The tide had turned against him. Never again would he experience the crowning glory of a triumphant campaign across the battlefields of Europe and don the victor's laurels.

THE BATTLEFIELDS TODAY

A visit to the battlefields of Aspern–Essling and Wagram will inevitably begin in Vienna. The starting point for any military enthusiast must be the Heeresgeschichtliches Museum (Museum of Army History). Built between 1850-56 as the Imperial Royal Artillery Arsenal, it now houses a superb military collection in a majestic setting.

Schönbrunn, the Habsburg's summer palace, is also worth a visit, as Napoleon occupied it prior to the battles at Aspern and Wagram. A statue of Charles, depicting the incident at Aspern with the standard, dominates the Heldenplatz. A visit to the austere Kaisergruft (Imperial Crypt) beneath the Capucins Kirche is also worthwhile; here lie the Habsburg

▶ *A statue of Charles dominates the Helden-platz in Vienna. This smaller version is on display in the Heeres-geschichtliches Museum. Both are the work of Anton von Fernhorn and depict the episode of Charles with the standard of IR15 (Zach) at Aspern–Essling. (HGM, Vienna).*

sarcophagii, including those of Charles and Francis, providing an interesting comparison with the inspiring tomb of Napoleon at Les Invalides.

The battlefields are best explored by car. Leaving Vienna, cross the Danube by the Reichsbrücke and follow Wagramer Strasse before turning right into Erzherzog Karl Strasse. This road will bring you into Aspern along the line followed by Hiller and Bellegarde. As you enter the village, the church, built on the site of that destroyed in the fighting, is to your right with its poignant memorial to the conflict. To the rear of the church is the Aspern Museum, which although small contains a fascinating collection relating to the battle. Normal opening times are limited, so it may be worth asking the Tourist Office to phone ahead and arrange an appointment. The village of Aspern, which witnessed such heavy fighting, has been rebuilt since the battle, but the houses are laid out on the old street lines, many of which bear names connected with the battle. A main road now links Aspern to Essling, but your view between the two villages is limited by a vast General Motors factory that has been built in the area. At Essling, while the walls of the Great Garden are no longer visible, there is no difficulty locating the granary, which still stands, defiantly jutting out to the north of the village, its massive walls as resistant to time as to the Austrian attacks. The granary has recently seen some renovation, but the iron door, complete with bullet holes, is still in place; there is a possibility that a part of the building may open to the public in the future as an extension of the Aspern Museum.

By following any of the roads north from Aspern or Essling you will cross the vast, open, flat plain of the Marchfeld on your way to Wagram. Just north of Raasdorf, by the side of the road, is a small rise covered in trees – it was from this spot that Napoleon observed the battle. At Deutsch-Wagram, Charles' headquarters building has been renovated and now houses a new museum; there is also a fine monument in the village. From Wagram, by following the sign to Markgrafneusiedl, you will be driving below the escarpment with the tree-lined Russbach on your right. Stop at any point and scramble up the Wagram and you will appreciate what an important position it is in an otherwise featureless terrain. At the far end of the road is the village of Markgrafneusiedl. Above the village on the escarpment stands the tower, which featured heavily in the fighting. Below, lying silently in the dark crypt beneath the village church are the countless bones of those who perished in the fierce struggle for supremacy at Markgrafneusiedl, which was to prove to be the beginning of the end of the war.

CHRONOLOGY

1808

9 June Austria authorizes the raising of the Landwehr.

21 July Surrender of Dupont's French force to a Spanish army at Bailen.

21 August Defeat of French force under Junot by Wellesley's Anglo-Portugese army at Vimiero.

September Napoleon authorizes the early enlistment of conscripts from 1810 and the previously exempt classes of 1806–1809.

27 September to 14 October Congress of Erfurt: Concerned by Austrian rearmament and the deteriorating situation in Spain, Napoleon extracts an agreement from Russia that it will support France if Austria becomes agressive.

25 October Napoleon arrives back in Paris.

29 October Napoleon leaves Paris for Spain.

5 November Napoleon takes command in Spain.

23 December Austria decides on war with France in the spring.

1809

16 January The Austrian chief of staff, Mayer, submits a plan of operation calling for a main thrust from Bohemia, north of the Danube, into Bavaria.

17 January Napoleon begins journey back to France, alerted by continued Austrian rearmament and intrigues in Paris.

24 January Napoleon arrives in Paris.

2 February Charles activates his new army corps system.

8 February Austria's decision for war receives final approval.

12 February Charles confirmed as supreme head of the army.

16 February Austrian army begins to move to assembly points.

20 February Mayer is replaced as Austrian chief of staff.

13 March Change of Austrian operational plan requires four corps to march south to new forming-up area south of the Danube.

17 March Napoleon appoints Berthier as his chief of staff in Germany.

10 April Austrian army crosses the border into Bavaria earlier than expected by the French. War begins.

13 April Napoleon leaves Paris.

17 April Napoleon arrives in Donauwörth, Bavaria, and assumes command.

19 April French III Corps defeats elements of Austrian III and IV Korps during the action at Teugn-Hausen.

20 April Battle of Abensberg.

21 April Battle of Landshut.

22 April Battle of Eggmühl.

24 April Battle of Neumarkt.

3 May Battle of Ebelsberg.

13 May Surrender of Vienna.

13 May French attempt to cross the Danube on to Schwarzen Lackenau repulsed.

20 May French troops begin to cross the Danube from Kaiser Ebersdorf.

21 May BATTLE OF ASPERN–ESSLING (First Day).

22 May BATTLE OF ASPERN–ESSLING (Second Day).

14 Jun Archduke John defeated at Battle of Raab.

4 July French army begins to cross the Danube on to the Marchfeld.

5 July BATTLE OF WAGRAM (First Day).

6 July BATTLE OF WAGRAM (Second Day).

10 July Battle of Znaim (First Day).

11 July Battle of Znaim (Second Day).

12 July Armistice signed.

23 July Archduke Charles resigns his command. Liechtenstein replaces him.

14 October The Peace of Schönbrunn is signed after lengthy negotiations.

A GUIDE TO FURTHER READING

ARNOLD, J. R. *Crisis on the Danube*, London, 1990. An entertaining, well written account but only dealing with early part of campaign.

BOWDEN, S. and Tarbox, C. *Armies on the Danube 1809*, Chicago, 1980. Organization of both armies and numerous orders of battle, although not always entirely accurate.

CHANDLER, D. G. *Dictionary of the Napoleonic Wars*, London, 1979. Excellent general background to people and events.

GILL, J. *With Eagles to Glory*, London and California, 1992. The authoritative account of the Rheinbund contingents in 1809.

PETRE, F. L. *Napoleon and the Archduke Charles*, 1909 (reprinted London, 1976). Extremely detailed account of the campaign. ROTHENBERG, G. E. *Napoleon's Great Adversaries*, London, 1982. Most comprehensive account of Austrian army available in English.

TRANIE, J. and Carmigniani, J. C. *Napoleon et L'Autriche – La Campagne de 1809*, Paris, 1979. French text, but contains superb collection of illustrations.

WOBER, F. I. *1809 - Schlacht bei Aspern und Essling*, Vienna, 1992. German text. The most detailed account of these battles, with excellent maps.

WARGAMING THE 1809 CAMPAIGN

Armies of toy soldiers are more pleasing to the eye than a rash of cardboard counters, but battles on the grand scale of Wagram are difficult to re-fight without resorting to 1/300th scale models – which is only one step away from counters. Attempts to stage such giant contests with 15mm (or, perish the thought, 25mm) figures have a depressing tendency to run out of time. For various reasons, most published sets of Napoleonic wargames rules are designed to re-fight battles at divisional or brigade level. This stems from what might be termed a 'bottom-up' approach, where the designer has worked out how to represent squadrons, batteries and battalions with a set number of figures, and scales his rules accordingly. It works well enough while a division of 12–16 battalions is on the table, but a 15mm scale re-creation of Wagram is likely to take as long as the real battle.

Fortunately, there are now several sets of published rules that take a 'top down' approach, making a re-fight of Wagram or Aspern-Essling entirely feasible. *Strategy & Tactics* issue 151 (May 1992) included Joseph Miranda's innovative boardgame of the battle of Friedland. He uses one-hour game turns; the smallest unit represented is the brigade, but most units are of divisional size. In a pleasing shift away from intricate boardgames like *La Bataille de la Moscowa* Miranda's Friedland game emphasizes command and control rather than the intricate tactical detail. Like Napoleon and the Archduke Charles at Wagram, you manoeuvre whole corps rather than fiddle about with individual battalions. This is equally applicable to the 1809 campaign, in which the fighting abilities of the Austrian troops came as a disagreeable surprise to Napoleon. His limited victory was secured not by having better battalions, but by having more of them, led by more capable generals.

In the UK, Peter Dennis and Cliff Knight have published *Napoleonic rules for a large scale wargame*. These are intended for 5mm or 2mm toy soldiers, but can be modified for use with existing armies of 15mm figures without difficulty. The authors rightly emphasise that if a player is supposed to be a corps or army commander, he will not be concerned with the deployment of specific battalions or batteries – he must concentrate on 'the big picture'. They also observe that with the very small ground scale (1: 4000 or 1 mm = 4 metres) players have an unrealistically accurate view of the battlefield. Looking down as if from a helicopter, they can see everything and react accordingly. If you can find some volunteers, use an umpire team to move the figures and try to restrict the players' view. Only then can the true confusion of the Napoleonic battlefield begin to be appreciated. If you do not have an umpire, represent units out of immediate contact with two markers, one real and one false. You might want to experiment with using figures instead of markers, placing a slip of paper under these units that shows their true identity.

In 1809 both commanders-in-chief positioned themselves in the thick of the fighting; Archduke Charles was wounded at Wagram and Napoleon at Regensberg (Ratisbon). The Archduke's personal bravery became part of Austrian military folklore, and there is no doubt that Napoleon's exposure to enemy fire was a deliberate risk, calculated to inspire the French army. Corps commanders also led from the front, and several paid for it with their lives. Whatever rules you employ to re-fight Wagram, personal intervention by senior officers should have an inspirational (if local) effect. It is up to the commanders to guess which sector of the battlefield is likely to prove decisive.

The 1809 campaign led to the largest battles yet known, and they were notable for some very heavy concentrations of artillery. Commanded as it was by a former gunner, the French army excelled at offensive artillery tactics. Most armies could deploy their artillery to reasonable effect on the defensive, but few equalled the French ability to bring its heavy guns forward, literally blasting a path for the French infantry. While still not as mobile as the French artillery, the Austrian gunners had improved dramatically since the dismal days of 1805. And, as Napoleon gloomily observed, when the Austrians finally retreated, most of their guns escaped with them.

The 1809 campaign involved a great deal of fighting in built-up areas: at Regensberg, Landshut, Aspern and Essling, French and Austrian infantrymen slugged it out with musket butt and bayonet. House-to-house fighting is not easy to represent in a figure game where a dozen toy soldiers represent an entire brigade, the sort of scale necessary to wargame a battle the size of Wagram. Perhaps the best solution is to resolve it boardgame-style by setting arbitrary limits on the number of men a village can be defended by, and assigning a defence value to the area. Even if an assault succeeds in capturing a village, it should leave the attackers temporarily disordered and vulnerable to an enemy counter-attack.

Still dressed in the eighteenth-century style uniforms they wore while fighting beside the Prussians in 1806, the Royal Saxon Army contributed more than 20,000 men to Napoleon's forces in 1809. Fighting for the first time as allies of the French, the Saxons were still wearing white, and their uniforms looked dangerously similar to those of the Austrians. As we have seen, the unfortunate Saxons were frequently shot at by both sides, and some regiments took to their heels as a result. Few sets of wargames rules allow for friendly troops to start firing at each other, but this sort of error was, and is, all too common in the chaos of the battlefield. Umpires have plenty of scope for injecting a little more confusion here; and it could equally well have worked in the Saxons' favour, with Austrian units not firing until too late because they identify them as friends.

Besides the great battles, the 1809 campaign is packed with dramatic incidents that can make excellent, and rather more manageable, wargames. Regensberg was strategically important because of its massive stone bridge over the Danube, and it was stormed twice in quick succession. On the first occasion, Davout left a single regiment, the 65th line, as a rearguard; commanded by the Marshal's cousin, the 65th was attacked by Kollowrat's corps of 20,000 men. This heroic regiment clung to its positions for over 48 hours, and was finally granted honours of war after sustaining fifty per cent casualties and running out of ammunition. Two days later, the French were back; now it was the turn of an Austrian rearguard to face a hail of heavy artillery, and repeated infantry charges eventually spearheaded by one of the Emperor's most aggressive Marshals and his staff. Landshut's bridge over the River Isar was also important, but it was made of wood and the Austrian rearguard managed to set it alight just as the French cavalry arrived. Again, the assault was led by one of Napoleon's praetorians – his A.D.C., Georges Mouton. Placing himself at the head of the grenadier company of the 17th line, he ran across the burning bridge while Austrian cannonballs threw up fountains of water

alongside. The grenadiers reached the Austrian barricades and stormed into the town.

All these heroics – up siege ladders and across burning bridges – cry out for a skirmish or role-playing game. What better objective for a 'death or glory' role-play game? Players can take the role of individual soldiers in the 17th line (or whichever regiment takes your fancy) and try to shine before the eyes of their Emperor as they brave a hail of Austrian musketry from the city walls.

Charles' strategy was partly determined by the limited bridging equipment at the Austrians' disposal. While engineers are often relegated to the sidelines during Napoleonic wargames, the fight for Lobau island and the bridging of the Danube could make an excellent mini-game in itself. The French engineers struggle to keep the bridge operational despite worsening weather, while the Austrians float down stone-filled barges to smash another hole in it. The French win by keeping the bridge open, allowing more reinforcements to cross over; the Austrians win by stopping them, or breaking the bridge while it is packed with troops or guns.

I have concentrated on the tactical games suggested by the Wagram campaign, but the military operations were dictated by *political* considerations. Napoleon miscalculated Austrian intentions, exposing his forces in southern Germany to Archduke Charles' offensive. His diplomatic effort was hampered by the treachery of his foreign minister, Talleyrand, who was secretly supplying information to the Austrians. See James Arnold's *Crisis on the Danube* for a concise introduction to the political machinations that lay behind the war. Although Napoleon laboured under a severe disadvantage because of his ministers' betrayal, the Austrian court was also divided. The Emperor Francis fell out with his brother Charles during the war, and, despite the Archduke's military record, he was removed from command. A full diplomatic game should include the British, with their usual offers of money and minor landings in the Low Countries. Historically, Napoleon managed to keep the Tsar out of the conflict, but another Austro-Russian alliance was always a possibility.

For a full simulation of the 1809 campaign, a diplomatic campaign could be carried on by mail, and the military actions fought out on a map or tabletop as they occur. The leading characters can appear in skirmish games as they lead storming parties into the breach, or in role-play games as they negotiate peace, secretly deal with the enemy or seduce the wives of enemy Marshals. The choice is yours.